Oliver Hind

GW01460095

and the 2nd Nottingham Company

of The Boys' Brigade

by Terence Woolley

Published By Terence Woolley Publications

Text copyright © 2013 Terence Woolley

All Rights Reserved

ISBN 978-0-9576599-0-2

Printed by Russell Press Ltd.
Russell House, Bulwell Lane,
Basford, Nottingham
NG6 OBT

Contents

Introduction

We are not here to play, to dream, to drift; we have hard work to do and loads to lift.

This is an account of people who dedicated themselves to improving the outlook of countless poor children otherwise condemned through ignorance and poverty to live miserable and degrading lives.

These people were almost all non-conformist Christians driven by a strong religious conviction and a compelling desire to bring their vision of heaven closer to earth. They were 'good Samaritans' who refused to pass along the other side of the road and ignore the plight of hundreds of thousands of vulnerable and defenceless children who suffered hardship and want.

Their answer was not charitable handouts, although they were generous in all respects, but in providing opportunities for the poor to break the shackles of destitution by advancement through education.

Oliver Watts Hind holds a place amongst these champions of impoverished children. But like his predecessors, he would not have succeeded in his ambitions without the support and efforts of many more dedicated, assiduous friends and helpers. This is as much their story as his.

The Trailblazers

The kingdom of god is like a mustard seed which is smaller than any seed in the ground at its sowing, but once sown, springs up and grows taller than any other plant and forms branches so large that birds can settle in its shade.

In the late decades of the eighteenth and early decades of the nineteenth century, the prospects for a child born into a poor family in the burgeoning cities of the mightiest commercial empire the world had seen were bleak. Cramped in unsanitary, unwholesome hovels, thinly clad in rags and hand-me-downs, malnourished, fed upon putrid water, it was little wonder that large numbers perished before reaching the age of five. And those fortunate enough to pass this milestone were condemned to spend most of their waking hours toiling, begging or stealing to gain a pittance to pay for their upkeep.

Industry flourished on the backs of children. Children laboured from twelve to sixteen hours a day, six days a week, often in stifling fumes and intense heat, their ears deafened by the roar and clatter of heavy machinery, their limbs deformed by forced unnatural postures, their eyes strained by staring in artificial light, their skins discoloured and blistered by lack of sunlight and toxic dust. The tiniest child in a cotton mill was forced to crawl beneath billowing machines, dodging swinging parts to avoid crushing death, to remove waste material. Mistakes or slacking were punished by forfeits and a licking from overseers, often keen for an excuse to deliver a thrashing.

Children laboured in factories. Children laboured down mines. In the cities, eyes stinging and choked with coal dust, blackened children clambered the inside of chimneys armed with a brush, coating themselves in their narrow dark passage with hot cinders and ash. On streets, children evaded heavy traffic to sweep a path through mud in the hope that scurrying, well-to-do pedestrians would impart a farthing to cross the road with unsullied shoes. Children ran messages. Children sold fruit, herbs, flowers, knick-knacks, flints, and lucifer-matches from trays. Children toiled at laborious and onerous chores. Children begged. Children thieved. Children died.

Diabolical treatment of defenceless children in the richest nation in the world was so much part-and-parcel of everyday life as to be blandly accepted by the majority as a matter of course. But there were those whose conscience recoiled at the evil heaped upon the most innocent and vulnerable in their midst.

There could be few places more vibrant and vital than late eighteenth century Portsmouth. The naval dockyard was expanding and a fleet was being built to outmatch the French. Ships were docked in all states of manufacture and repair. War vessels with heaving canvas sails rigged to tall masts and lines of gun ports shielding the protruding muzzle of heavy cannon came and left with the ebb and flow of every tide. The docks were congested day and night with traffic, sailors, and workmen of all manner of trades. Shanties and raucous laughter issued from quayside taverns. The streets were alive with hawkers, entertainers, and noisy, off-duty mariners.

Eager and willing by nature and pitched into this heady turmoil as apprentice shipwright at the age of twelve, John Pounds' future looked assured until, three years into his apprenticeship, his hopes and body were both shattered when he fell into a dry dock. Surviving the fall, his broken bones set as best they might and he was left a cripple for life.

But John's spirit was irrepressible. He used his drawn-out months of convalescence learning to read and write and broadening his education. When able to walk, albeit almost bent double, he learned to be a cobbler.

He shared a walking impediment with a nephew, Johnnie, who had been born with deformed feet. Rather than breaking and realigning the bones, a painful and hazardous procedure, John took care of the boy and made him a special pair of boots to help straighten his feet as he grew.

Watching his young nephew play with friends in his workshop inspired the young cobbler to share with the children what he had learned while he was convalescing. He taught them to read and write and simple arithmetic and was sufficiently buoyed by his success that he scoured the streets of Portsmouth looking for more impoverished children to teach. Soon he had over 40 pupils. Beyond the basics, he taught them to mend clothes, cook and various crafts such as toy making. His reputation spread far and wide as the crippled teacher of poor children.

At about the same time as John Pounds was establishing a free school for destitute children in Portsmouth, Robert Raikes, a newspaper publisher in Gloucester, initiated the Sunday School movement to teach bible studies and basic education to children who worked long hours on the none-Sabbath days. Using the Bible as a text book, he taught children how to read and write. It was a popular approach and the Sunday School movement soon gathered pace and spread to all parts of the country.

But as families drifted from shire to city in a desperate migration in search of work, church going traditions were breaking down. Urban streets, crowded with discontented, hungry adults and outcast waifs and urchins, became a festering ground for unruliness and criminality. Left to their own devices and following the example of disreputable adults, children often sank into a life of depravity and crime. In an attempt to counter this process, in 1798 Thomas Cranfield, a Congregational Sunday School teacher from Hackney, opened a free school for poor children in Kent Street near London bridge. Over the following decades he built up an organization of nineteen schools across the slums of London.

While not the first or only ones to address the plight of destitute children, the achievements of John Pounds, Robert Raikes, and Thomas Cranfield struck a chord that others in the crowded, industrial conurbations were to follow. More free schools for the poor were started by churches and staffed by volunteers and in 1835 the newly formed London City Mission established the Ragged School movement, hiring staff to assist the poor with a wide range of charitable help ranging from clothing to basic education.

Educating hitherto uncontrolled children in rudimentary and badly provisioned rooms in congested slums where they were generally regarded with suspicion and derision was difficult and sometimes dangerous for fledgling teachers. Unruly children disrupted lessons and school rooms were sometimes raided by a disgruntled mob and ransacked. Unprotected teachers were quite often assaulted. But, thanks to their dedication and courage, the Ragged School movement flourished.

Towards the end of his life in 1839, it is possible that John Pounds and children he had taught may have enjoyed instalments of the first novels of Charles Dickens, a fellow native of Portsmouth. The impact of his writing on shaping the social conscience of the nation about this time was immeasurable. Together with a number of wealthy benefactors, he took an interest in the development of the Ragged School movement.

In 1844, political reformer Anthony Ashley-Cooper inaugurated the Ragged School Union. Three years later, having set up a Ragged School in Edinburgh, Thomas Guthrie published a "Plea for Ragged Schools" and, in 1852, as a result of lobbying by the Ragged Schools movement, a parliamentary committee was set up to examine the use of education to improve conditions and reduce juvenile crime. By this time, hundreds of free schools for the poor, teaching reading, writing, arithmetic, Bible studies and crafts such as clothing repair and cobbling, had been established throughout the length and breadth of Britain.

George Williams moved from rural Somerset to London at the age of fifteen to work as an apprentice to a draper. He lived at his place of work and worked long hours but in snatches of leisure time afforded him he was appalled by the squalor and deprivation in which many families lived in the capital city and the lack of amenities to encourage a healthy lifestyle. In 1844, at the age of twenty three he founded the Young Men's Christian Association (YMCA) with the purpose of "the improving of the spiritual condition of young men engaged in the drapery, embroidery, and other trades." His aim was to put Christian principles into practice by encouraging the development of a healthy "body, mind and spirit" amongst young men. Popular from the outset, the movement soon spread around other British cities and then abroad. It staged its first world conference in Paris in 1855.

Arriving in London from Dublin in 1866 as a medical student with the intention of travelling to China as a missionary, Thomas Barnardo found himself a helpless witness to a cholera epidemic. Sweeping through the overcrowded East End of the city, it killed over three thousand and left many more destitute and homeless. He changed his plans.

Encouraged by Anthony Ashley-Cooper, he first became involved in the Ragged School movement. Then in 1870, he opened a home for homeless boys. Others followed. His object was to search and take in waifs and strays, to feed, clothe and educate. Over the next decades he rescued thousands of homeless children and equipped them with a grounding of education sufficient to allow them to find work and live honest lives.

National hero and champion of the empire, Charles George Gordon, was quartered at Gravesend from 1865 to 1871. A man of strong Christian faith, he assisted at the Ragged School and set aside rooms in his home to teach poor children from the area. When he was killed defending Khartoum in 1885, the Gordon Boys' Homes were founded as a memorial to his name. The object of the homes was to accommodate and teach destitute boys between the ages of thirteen to seventeen in trades such as tailoring, shoemaking, carpentry, engineering, gardening, cooking, baking and blacksmithing. The boys were kitted with a military-style uniform, ranked from private to colour-sergeant, attended drill and Bible lessons, and were summoned to meals by bugle call.

Ragged Schools and Barnardo's and Gordon Boys' Homes proved that children taken from squalid slums could be taught to raise themselves above a life of wretched poverty. Instilled with a sense of achievement and self-respect and taught a trade, countless escaped the cycle of destitution and degradation to live wholesome and fulfilling lives.

By reducing the number of hours children were allowed to work, mid eighteenth century Factory Reform Acts (spearheaded, amongst others, by Anthony Ashley-Cooper, president of the Ragged School Union) unintentionally led to a surge of mischief and petty crime as unrestrained children were set loose on the streets for longer periods of time. Voices still vehemently arguing that universal education would only stimulate expectations beyond what was possible and lead to revolution became eclipsed by the more enlightened argument that the security and prosperity of all would benefit from educating the whole population bolstered by a general plea to take children off the streets by whatever means. Starting with the 1870 Education Act, a series of Parliamentary Acts required Local Government to provide free education to all children between the ages of five and ten, extended to thirteen with the introduction of Local Education Authorities in 1902. The Ragged Schools movement had fulfilled its purpose and was absorbed or displaced by state run schools.

But these changes took time to settle in and were not always welcome to poor families whose children could no longer work and bring home a wage.

William Alexander Smith

Put the boy first.

William Alexander Smith was born in Thurso, the most northerly town in mainland Britain, on 27th of October 1854. At that time there was no train link to Wick, the nearest town, some twenty miles away, and, isolated between a highland wilderness and capricious winds and tides of the northern Atlantic, the people of this small community had little choice but to be resilient, resourceful, and self-reliant.

As a child, William would have witnessed the fishing fleet, anchored overnight in the sheltered waters of the river Thurso, take to the swelling ocean to harvest their daily catch and the lifeline ferry, loaded with vital supplies, steering a buffeted course through choppy seas between Scrabster harbour and the Orkney Islands. Sunday prayers for neighbours lost at sea would not have been infrequent.

William's father fought in the South Africa 'Kaffir War' of 1849 as a Major in the 7th Dragoon Guards; his grandfather fought in the 78th Highlander Regiment in the Napoleonic wars. Living in Pennyland House, overlooking Thurso Bay and the Pentland Firth, in a household where military service and pride of accomplishment were held in high esteem, William grew to be a serious minded young man with a strong sense of integrity and responsibility.

Tragedy struck and changed the course of his life when, at the age of thirteen, news arrived that his father had died while on a business trip in China. His mother's brother ran a family soft goods wholesaling and exporting business,

Alex. Fraser & Co., in Glasgow. William moved to live with his uncle and joined the firm in 1869 as a junior clerk.

For a young man brought up in a closely-knit community in a small town fed by a clean river and invigorated by fresh air breezing across the northern ocean, the difference in his environment could hardly have been more stark. Glasgow, the second largest city in the kingdom, was a scene of heavy industry, billowing fumes, grinding noise, and clogging traffic. The river was wide, busy with shipping, and filthy; the air reeked with a stench of bad sanitation mingled with the smell of smelting, malting, tanning, dyeing, and all manner of industry; the night streets in the centre of the city and docks were a bewildering maelstrom of prostitution, drunken brawling and crime.

Fortunately, staying with his uncle, William lived some distance from the raucous hullabaloo of the city centre. When old enough, he joined the Glasgow YMCA where he could share camaraderie with other young men of similar temperament and outward-bound interests and, on reaching the age of nineteen, he enlisted with the 1st Lanarkshire Rifle Volunteers. A year later he joined the Free College Church where in 1874 he set up his own branch of the YMCA.

In 1877 he gained a commission of Lieutenant in the Rifle Volunteers after which his Saturday afternoons were spent drilling soldiers on a parade ground.

He also became Secretary of the Sunday School Teachers' Society and, on Sundays, gave Sunday School lessons to children in the Free College Church Mission Hall in North Woodside Road, close to where he lived.

As time progressed, he was disturbed by the striking comparison between his Saturday drill parade, where the soldiers behaved impeccably, and his Sunday School class which was peppered with annoying interruptions, some of the older boys being particularly restless and fidgety.

Boys of the Glasgow Foundry Boys' Religious Society, an organisation in which poor boys were taught basic education, religious instruction and drill, had been marching proudly behind flute and drum on Sunday Church parade since 1865. The boys presented themselves well and behaved respectfully during the church service.

Coalescing his thoughts and experiences in the YMCA and the Rifle Volunteers and with the example of the Glasgow Foundry Boys' Religious Society to hand, William conceived the notion of a Boys' Brigade.

On the 4th of October 1883, ably supported by two YMCA friends and fellow Sunday School teachers, brothers James and John Hill, he invited boys from his Sunday School to form the 1st Glasgow Company. His object was 'the advancement of Christ's kingdom among boys and the promotion of habits of reverence, discipline, self-respect, and all that tends towards a true Christian manliness'.

It was a time of patriotism and pride in the British Empire. The Queen had recently been crowned Empress of India. Britain ruled the waves. Vast swathes of global maps were shaded British pink. The defence of Rorke's Drift against Zulus and General Gordon's heroic stand at Khartoum swelled the public imagination. In this environment, the concept of a Boys' Brigade met with an enthusiastic response. Fifty nine boys between the age of twelve and sixteen were eager to join.

Discipline was rigorous and uncompromising from the outset. Boys were expected to set an example of good conduct. No boy was allowed to attend if late on parade. Boys were not allowed to miss more than one drill parade without compelling reason. Numbers fell to thirty-five.

But by the end of the season William saw a measure of success in what he had created and consolidated his ideas. He established a hierarchy of command similar to his Rifle Volunteers, conceived a basic, inexpensive uniform, and formulated rules. He divided the Company into six squads and appointed two Sergeants, two Corporals and two Lance-Corporals.

It worked well. In large measure, the boys regulated themselves and at Sunday Bible Class there was quietness, attention and reverence during prayer.

In March 1884, William married his long-time sweetheart, Amelia Sutherland, the daughter of a Presbyterian chaplain, and moved into a house close to the Mission Hall where he ran his Company. The Company held its first summer camp at Tighnabruaich in 1886 and thereafter, an annual camp was a central feature of the summer season.

Like the YMCA before it, The Boys' Brigade movement spread quickly throughout Great Britain and then overseas. Heavily engaged in correspondence with fledgling Companies, William gave up his business career to become full-time Secretary of The Boys' Brigade in 1887. He wrote 'How to Form and Conduct a Company' and edited The Boys' Brigade Gazette. For the rest, he was busy communicating with the many Companies and Battalions that were being established throughout the world.

He was knighted for his services to children in 1909 and died on 10 May 1914, the day after a London Albert Hall Demonstration in front of Prince Alexander of Teck and a full audience of parents, friends, and supporters. By this time The Boy's Brigade was the largest youth movement in the world.

The Boys' Brigade

Sure and Stedfast.

William Alexander Smith's booklet, 'How to Form and Conduct a Company' defined the purpose, structure and activities of The Boys' Brigade.

Built upon pillars of religion and discipline, all Companies were to meet once a week for a parade night and each Sunday for a Bible class. Every boy was expected to be present on both occasions. Beyond this, boys were encouraged to participate in sports, gymnastics, first-aid, music, crafts, signalling, wayfaring, swimming and life saving, and games. For a period, Lieutenant-General Robert Baden-Powell, hero of the siege of Mafeking and author of 'Aids to Scouting' and 'Scouting for Boys', introduced a scouting class (it proved so overwhelmingly popular he hived off to form a separate popular movement in 1907).

The hierarchy of The Boys' Brigade was modelled upon the armed services. A Company was headed by a Captain who was supported by Warrant Officers and Lieutenants. It was open to boys between the ages of twelve and seventeen who were ordered into squads. New boys started as Privates but, by application, good-conduct, and accomplishment could rise through the ranks to Lance-Corporal, Corporal, Sergeant, Colour-Sergeant, and Staff-Sergeant. Each rank entailed privileges and responsibilities. If there was more than one Company in a town or district, they would form a Battalion and their would be Battalion competitions and an annual demonstration and Church Parade.

The uniform was simple to avoid undue expense. Up to the rank of Sergeant, boys wore a pillbox cap tilted to the right side of the head and held in place by a chin strap. The cap was black with two encircling, narrow white bands and topped with a small central white button. A white haversack worn across the right shoulder was held at the waist on the left hip by a leather belt that had a central, round, brass buckle. A Sergeant was distinguished by a peak cap worn straight on the head and a shoulder belt over the left shoulder and crossing the haversack. Staff-Sergeants wore a field service cap worn on one side of the head and carried a short cane. Officers wore a glengarry cap with crest. A shining silver Company number was worn in the centre of pillbox caps and peak caps between the narrow white bands and in a prominent position on field service caps.

It went without saying that clothes were tidy, shoes were squeaky clean, hats were brushed of all blemish, haversacks were perfectly starched and ironed, leather belts were well polished, and badges and buckles shone in the sunlight like burnished silver and gold.

Boys were awarded a button-hole 'anchor' badge after three months and a service badge after each year. They were awarded certificates and badges to denote their progress in the various disciplines in which they took part. These were presented at a special prize giving ceremony which normally formed part of an annual demonstration. Badges were worn in a fixed arrangement between shoulder and elbow on both arms. NCOs wore chevron stripes denoting their rank on the right arm below their badges.

Each session started in early Autumn and finished in mid Summer and included The Boys' Brigade Week (a week set aside for fund raising to support the functions of The Boys' Brigade), an annual Company and Battalion demonstration, a Battalion Parade, and a summer camp.

The demonstration took the form of a show and provided an opportunity for boys to display their skills and entertain parents and friends. The band played while the audience settled in their seats. An erect Drill-Sergeant barked instructions and stepped a squad of immaculately presented boys through a series of marching manoeuvres. The gymnast team performed breath-taking feats on a wooden horse. A volunteer was trussed in an arm sling and leg splints and carried away on a stretcher by the first-aid team. The band played a medley from a popular operetta. Agile boys formed pyramids and performed coordinated tumbling feats. Boys demonstrated their table tennis and sparring skills. The evening culminated in the Captain's speech, in which he highlighted achievements of the past year and set out milestones for the next, followed by a prize giving ceremony where boys stepped forward to receive certificates and badges from an honoured guest. The evening closed with a dramatic finale in which all boys participated and a parting prayer.

The best acts at Company level featured in a Battalion demonstration held at a prominent venue in the town or city. The very best acts featured in the national demonstration, staged at the Royal Albert Hall in London.

At the Battalion Parade, Companies marched to a church service after which they mustered for a march past a prominent salute taker. Hearing the jangle of approaching bands, spectators and well-wishers lined the streets to watch each Company file past. The sound of drum, pipe, brass, and bugle reverberating between buildings blended into an echoing cacophony between companies. At the march past, eyes turned to honour the salute-taker. Finally, the companies divided and marched to their places of dismissal.

The summer camp was the icing on the cake for which boys paid weekly instalments from their pocket money. Only boys who attended and behaved well at drill parades and Bible class were allowed to take part (a strong inducement for good behaviour). For some it was their only holiday.

It required a lot of pre-planning to provide transport, equipment, and provisions. A good cook was essential. A fatigue party normally set out a few days in advance to erect tents and prepare the ground.

Boys were allocated to tents in a similar way as they were to squads, each tent being a mix of senior and junior boys. On arriving, they would be issued with a palliasse and pillow and directed to a pile of straw. When they had settled in, a bugle call would invite them to the cookhouse where they would be told the programme and orderly rota for the week.

The daily routine was rigorous. Aroused at what seemed the crack of dawn by bugle reveille, all shuffled to an ablution centre where they would wash and brush their teeth in icy cold water. This might be followed by an early-morning swimming parade. They would then be summoned by clarion call to the cookhouse where they would feast upon porridge and tea, clean their crockery and utensils, and check the day's itinerary posted on the cookhouse wall.

In mid-morning there was a tent inspection. Palliasses were folded in as orderly fashion as possible, in front of the tent on fine days, otherwise, in situ. Blankets, folded by two boys holding each one end (two folds lengthways, dropping the final fold and gathering on the opposite side, the blanket owner striding three steps to his helpmate folding crosswise at a third and two thirds intervals), were placed neatly on the palliasse and topped with the pillow. Sparkling crockery and cutlery and a Bible were lodged neatly on top of the pile. This done, the boys stood in uniform against their pile to await inspection. Officers-of-the-day checked that the tent was well pegged and tidy, satisfied themselves that the boys were clean, correctly attired and shoes were polished, probed blanket piles that look suspiciously unstable, and made mysterious notes before moving on to the next tent. At the end, a tent was awarded a star for the day. Occupants of the worst tent were in danger of having to join the orderlies in the daily chore of spud-bashing.

Two hours of sport later, a bugle call summoned all to the cookhouse to enjoy healthy portions of boiled beef and mashed potatoes followed by spotted-dick.

The afternoon was taken up with inter-tent football and cricket matches, swimming, and other games. There were occasional outings to local areas of interest and, depending upon the distance, there may have been an open day to allow parents to see how well their children were faring.

After a tea of bread and jam and having spruced themselves up for a visit to the local attractions, boys queued before the camp treasurer to extract money from their saved-up stash. A little advice may have been offered about not spending it all in the first two days and the money was handed over and the transaction recorded.

All back before lights-out, the day finished with a cocoa supper, a last-post bugle call, whispering in the dark, and a sound sleep.

The last day was often reserved for a special sports day or treasure hunt.

The home trip was a time of mixed feelings; disappointment that the adventure and escapades had come to an end mingled with thoughts of a return to home cooking and a comfortable bed. Many had shared unforgettable moments and formed friendships that would last a lifetime.

The adventure begins here.

Walking from Trent Bridge along Bridgford Road in Nottingham, the last and most southerly entrance gates to the Trent Bridge Cricket Ground are called the John Auger Dixon Memorial Gates. A plaque set in the wall on the left hand side of the gates commemorates this famous and highly popular sportsman of the late nineteenth century.

John Dixon played cricket for Nottinghamshire as batsman (top score 268 not out against Sussex) and medium-paced bowler (best bowling 5 wickets for 28 runs) from 1882 to 1905. He was the team Captain for ten years from 1889. In one match against Leicester, he scored 126 not out and took 9 wickets. He also played football on the left wing for Notts County (scoring 16 goals in 61 appearances) and in March 1885 played for England in a match against Wales (England 1 Wales 1). After retiring as a cricket player, he remained a member of Nottinghamshire County Cricket Club Committee and was for a time an England Test Match Team Selector. Away from sport, he was a partner in his family clothing business, Dixon and Parker. Later in life, was appointed Justice of the Peace and elected to the board of a number of companies, including the Nottingham Building Society.

A devout churchgoer and a man of strong religious belief, at the height of his sporting achievements, he became a friend and shared ideas with Llewellyn Henry Gwynne, a curate at St. Andrew's Church on Mansfield Road, Nottingham.

Llewellyn had played centre-forward for Derby County Football Club. He was appointed vicar of Emmanuel Church, not far from St. Andrew's Church, on Woodborough Road, Nottingham, in 1892. In 1899, fired by the example of General Gordon and having read an appeal by the Church Missionary Society for missionaries to go to Sudan, he set up a mission in Khartoum and was appointed Archdeacon for the Sudan in 1905 and Bishop of Khartoum in 1908. He returned to Britain to act as Chaplain to the army at the outbreak of the First World War and was appointed Deputy Chaplain-General to the army in France in July 1915. At the end of the war he resumed his calling in the Middle-East and was appointed Bishop of Egypt and Sudan in 1920.

John Dixon and Llewellyn Gwynne introduced The Boys' Brigade to Nottingham in 1888 forming the 1st Nottingham Company which met at the St. Andrew's Church Mission Room in Bullivant Street, off Alfred Street Central. Four years later, John Dixon formed a Nottingham Battalion of which he was the first President. By the end of the 1892/1893 session, ten Companies had enrolled.

The 2nd Nottingham Company was formed in connection with St James Church, which stood on St. James Terrace, opposite Rutland Street, now abridged to Rutland Square, close to the site where King Charles 1st raised his standard on August 25th 1642 to start the English civil war. The Company enrolled into the Nottingham Battalion in 1894.

Provided with headquarters in Rutland Street, the Company admitted a small membership of boys at weekly meetings for the next eleven years.

Oliver Watts Hind

Champion of boys.

Jesse Hind was born in 1842 in Walker Street, Sneinton, Nottingham, the second son of William Hind and wife Ann (born Ann Ashover).

William Hind managed a small joiner and cabinet making business. As his eldest son, it would have been natural for Jesse to join the family business, but this he left to his brother, Enoch. His intellect and talents led him in a different direction. Educated at the High Pavement Sunday School, he gained sufficient mastery of the subjects taught as to serve for a time as teacher. Afterwards, to take full advantage of his academic aptitude, he decided upon a career in law and became an articled solicitor's clerk with the firm Enfield and Dowson. Applying himself assiduously, he gained his articles and a reputation as the 'Law Walking Dictionary' for his comprehensive knowledge of case law.

Highly impressed by the diligence and assuredness of this bright newcomer to the profession, Arthur Wells, a well-established, successful solicitor, offered Jesse a partnership and they formed the firm Wells and Hind based at offices in Fletcher Gate, Nottingham. Here, built upon a foundation of integrity and reliability, Jesse became a prominent solicitor. By the time the Nottinghamshire County Council was formed in 1889, he was regarded as the most capable and suitable member of the legal profession in the county and was invited to take the position of First Clerk to the Council. He was later appointed Clerk of the Peace for the County and a Justice of the Peace. He became solicitor for many of the most prominent businesses in Nottingham including the Boots Company and the Raleigh Bicycle Company.

Jesse married Eliza Watts on March the 18th 1865. They had seven children. Their first, Edward Watts, born in the summer of 1865, sadly died in the late summer of 1873, aged eight. Their second child, Jesse William, was born in the late summer of 1866. He was followed by Edith May, born in the summer of 1870, Oliver Watts, born in the winter of 1873, Ethel Maud, born in the summer or 1875, Lawrence Arthur, born in the winter of 1877, and Harold Ashover, born in the winter of 1879.

Jesse had a strong Christian faith and sense of civic duty. Beyond his family life and striking legal career, he devoted a great deal of time to voluntary work. From an early age he was a member of the North Midland Sunday School Association of which he was, for a time, the President. He was elected to the council of the Presbyterian and Unitarian Association. He became a volunteer in the Robin Hood Rifles. He and his wife were members of the committee of the Nottingham Day Nursery and Orphanage (Eliza played an active part in fund raising events; Jesse was at one time President). From its inception in 1880, both were on the committee of the Nottinghamshire Branch of the Women's Suffrage Movement (Eliza was at one time the treasurer). Jesse was on the committee of the Children's Hospital and the Notts Throat and Ear Hospital, once again, for a time, as President. He became actively involved in politics becoming Honorary Secretary of the North Notts Liberal Association, Chairman of the West Nottingham Liberal Association, and agent for prospective Liberal M.P.s. He was invited onto the board of directors of several ventures including the Nottingham House and Land Company incorporated in 1878 and the Nottingham Joint Stock Bank.

The family home life was equally intense. Social and fund raising events were frequent; cricket was a favourite summer sport; Eliza was an enthusiastic horse rider in the local hunt.

Raised in such a dynamic environment, it was no surprise that all four sons should follow the example of their illustrious father and enter a legal career.

Oliver was awarded a B.A. degree in law at Trinity Hall, Cambridge, in December 1894 after which he joined the family firm of Wells and Hind with his father and elder brother, Jesse, as a solicitor. In June 1899, he was awarded an LL.M, Master of Laws at Cambridge.

By 1890, the family home was Papplewick Grange and for a number of years Oliver undertook the Captaincy of the Linby and Papplewick Cricket Team and took part with his mother and sisters in the local hunt. Following the example of his father, he accepted a commission in the territorial army and, in 1898, joined both parents on the committee of the Nottingham Day Nursery and Orphanage.

He was particularly interested in the plight of disadvantaged children.

As a solicitor, he saw plenty of examples of children from poor backgrounds getting entangled in petty crime. Their lives blighted at an early stage, it was not uncommon for them to be drawn into ever more desperate criminal pursuits and face longer terms in prison.

Oliver had been raised in a Christian household where it was a fundamental belief that all are born equal and have intrinsically good qualities but that, prey to the corrosive effects of want, degradation and ignorance, the poor are susceptible to falling into bad and sometimes criminal habits. Like the pioneers of the Ragged School movement, he saw a cycle of poverty and wretchedness perpetuated by poor education.

Living conditions for the poor of Nottingham had improved markedly over the nineteenth century. In the mid-to-late 1890's, a major slum conurbation bounded by Parliament Street, Mansfield Road, and Glasshouse Street was demolished to make way for the Victoria Railway Station. Many of the thousands of families who were displaced moved into modern terraced housing in St. Anns, Sneinton, Lenton, Radford, and the Meadows. These houses were not shared with other families, were supplied with clean water and gas lighting and had an outside private water closet toilet.

But while living conditions had improved, there was still a great amount of poverty and economic uncertainty amongst working class families.

Investment in universal education had been inadequate to meet the demands of the Education Acts of 1870, 1892 and 1902 to provide free primary and secondary education for all from the ages of five to thirteen. Accommodation was spartan and teachers, faced with large classes of unwilling, sometimes disruptive children, were often ill-prepared and unsuited to fulfil the demands placed upon them. As a result, many children saw schooling as nothing more than an irksome imposition, behaved badly, and left school barely more knowledgeable than when they had arrived.

Oliver Hind saw these children trapped by their ignorance to a life of drudgery and insecurity. He was convinced that the hours they squandered loitering in the streets and involving themselves in mischievous escapades would be much better employed in activities that would cultivate their talents and develop their minds; that with direction and application, they could break the cycle of poverty and live useful and fulfilling lives.

He was aware of the work and successes of the Thomas Barnardo's and General Gordon Boys' Homes in this respect and, having served for ten years as an Officer in the 1st Nottinghamshire Volunteer Rifle Corps, understood the value of discipline in developing an esprit-de-corps amongst a body of men. In 1901, he accepted an invitation to become an Officer in the 18th Nottingham Company of The Boys' Brigade at Hucknall, close to his Papplewick home.

By the time the Hind family moved from Papplewick Grange to Edwalton Hall in 1905, Oliver had gained four years of experience as a Boys' Brigade Officer at Hucknall.

He took command of the 2nd Nottingham Company in Rutland Street. It was a Company of seventeen boys meeting weekly.

His ambition was to combine the pillars of religion and discipline that underpinned The Boys' Brigade with opportunities that would help disadvantaged boys prosper in life.

Introducing Alfred Davidson, a steadfast and dependable colleague from the territorial army, as his second in command, he initiated nightly meetings where the boys could take part in creative activities. The membership of the Company increased to a point where it outgrew the space available at Rutland Street. He looked around for more appropriate accommodation.

The Dakeyne Street Lads' Club (DAKO)

Be strong, quit you like men.

The Nottingham General Lunatic Asylum was a large building opened in 1811 at the top of what is now the King Edward Park, off Carlton Road, Sneinton (close to Walker Street where Jesse Hind was born). For most of the nineteenth century it was home to people diagnosed as lunatics and weak-minded paupers. In 1880, the clinically insane were transferred to the new Mapperley Hospital leaving only the paupers who were eventually transferred to Saxondale Hospital in 1902.

Oliver Hind thought this capacious, vacant building located in the centre of an area of honest, hard-working, poor people, ideally suited his purpose.

Walls that separated asylum cells were knocked down, supporting walls and ceilings were reinforced, and rooms were remodelled and decorated. The cost of acquiring and converting the building was the first of a long line of large expenses he was to bear implementing his plans for a boys' club. Rooms were furnished to accommodate games, gymnastics, drill, work shops, class rooms and a brass band. There was a library comprising of over 350 books, a sweet shop, baths, and separate rooms allocated for junior and old boys.

Calling upon his network of friends and supporters to help fulfil his ambitions, an NCO's room was furnished from a £2,000 endowment fund invested by the executors of Thomas George Langham. Later, mainly through the kindness of hosiery manufacturer and philanthropist, John William Lamb (the John William Lamb Charity provides assistance for elderly and needy people in Nottingham to this day), an athletic ground covering over seven acres was acquired at Trent Lane. This provided football and cricket pitches and had a river frontage where boys could bathe, row, and fish.

The curtain wall that surrounded the asylum was removed and the grounds were opened to the public and named the King Edward Park. Access to the Club was from Dakeyne Street which ran alongside the park. An inscription above the entrance porch, repeated in large letters in the main games room, proclaimed the Club motto, 'Be strong, quit you like men'.

The conversion work was completed and the Club opened on November 11th, 1907. It was named the Dakeyne Street Lads' Club, soon popularly shortened to DAKO.

Boys were admitted according to the regulations of The Boys' Brigade. All were required to equip themselves with the appropriate uniform and attend a weekly Bible class and drill parade. There were nightly meetings in which boys were encouraged to take part in Boys' Brigade activities, such as gymnastics, first-aid, scouting, a silver band, games, and various team sports.

But, beyond this, Oliver Hind was determined to provide educational opportunities for his Club members. He devised a scheme with the local Education Committee to provide specialist instructors to teach academic and craft subjects, such as reading, writing and composition, shorthand, arithmetic, book-keeping, history, geography, crafts, woodwork and shoe repair. The Dakeyne Street Lads' Club became an official Evening Continuation School under the control of the Education Committee and under Government inspection. On reaching school leaving age, boys had to notify the Education Office of the Education Committee if they wished to attend the Dakeyne Street Evening School. It soon had the highest average attendance of any evening school in Nottingham.

Oliver Hind had established a radically new kind of club and the results of his work drew attention throughout the youth club world. Others followed his example. In 1909, Stephen Hetley Pearson, an Officer at the Dakeyne Street Lads' Club, took over the Captaincy of the 17th Company at Beeston. Reorganising and reforming it along the Dakeyne Street lines, he created the Beeston Lads' Club, which grew in strength to three hundred members (Stephen and twenty seven old boys from his Club were amongst the first to enlist to fight for their country at the outbreak of the First World War; Stephen and 42 old boys of the Club lost their lives in the conflict).

With a membership of three to four hundred boys, the Dakeyne Street Lads' Club became the largest Company of the largest youth movement in the world.

As the Club Superintendent, Alfred Davidson resided with his family in a residential section of the Dakeyne Street premises. His wife, Alice Margaret, inaugurated a mothers' society which met on Monday afternoons where they were entertained by musical recitals and speakers on various subjects after which they were served tea and a bun for 2d. At times, the society attracted 300 mothers.

Prominent in team sports, fielding three football teams, the 2nd Nottingham Company played a significant part in Battalion inter-Company competitions and at annual demonstrations held at venues such as the Mechanics Hall, the Albert Hall, the Hippodrome, and the Empire Theatre. The annual camp, sometimes shared with other Companies, attracted three to four hundred boys.

With so much activity going on, boys were disappointed to leave at the age of seventeen. From 1909, a room was set aside to allow them to continue their association with the Club as old boys. They were provided with games tables and ran sports teams. In return, they were expected to attend the Sunday Bible class and assist at camps. The arrangement was given official status in 1912 with the inauguration of the Dakeyne Street Old Boys' Association.

During this period, the work of Oliver Hind was prolific. Not only did he dedicate a great deal of time into running and developing his Club, but from 1906 he took on the responsibility of Battalion President where he carried out his duties with vigour and success.

In April 1912, the founder of The Boys' Brigade, Sir William Alexander Smith, paid a visit to the Nottingham Battalion. He was entertained at the annual Battalion demonstration, which he said was one of the best provincial displays he had ever seen, and the following evening, having spent the day visiting various boys' clubs in the city, he attended an Officers' conference held at the invitation of the Battalion President, Oliver Hind, at the Dakeyne Street Lads' Club. In a speech he gave to the meeting, he stated that he found the work being done in Nottingham a revelation and that he was highly impressed by the example at Dakeyne Street.

Oliver Hind ended his term as Battalion President in 1913 and became the representative for the North Midlands on the governing body of The Boys' Brigade. He passed the Battalion Presidency to his long-standing colleague and friend, Richard Henry Swain, J.P.

Richard Swain was a successful business man in the lace drying and dressing industry. He had formed the 8th Nottingham Company in West Bridgford in 1897 and was the Company Captain for more than thirty years. In 1916, he was the Sheriff of Nottingham. He later became a co-director of the Nottingham Building Society alongside close colleague and first President of the Battalion, John Auger Dixon. He carried out the functions of Battalion President with distinction for 32 years.

To commemorate the transfer of presidency, a swimming gala was arranged at Victoria Baths at which there was a water polo match between teams captained by Oliver Hind and Richard Swain.

In April the following year, an assembly of Officers was organised to meet at the Arboretum Rooms where the guest for the evening was Lord Guthrie, the President of The Boys' Brigade. The main purpose of the meeting was acknowledged by Richard Swain when he requested Lord Guthrie to present Oliver Hind with a silver salver dish upon which was engraved the names of the Officers. It was said to be not only a token of the esteem and regard with which all Officers of the Battalion held Oliver Hind, but also an expression of the gratitude for his successful period as Battalion President, during which the number of Officers and boys almost doubled, and for his remarkable work at the Dakeyne Street Lads' Club.

A porch entrance leads into the games room at the end of which is a spiral staircase to the upper drill hall. The door next to the staircase opens upon a flight of steps descending to a basement reading room. The second door is to the Captain's office. A passage opposite the iron staircase provides access to other parts of the building. The two doors on the right of the games room lead into the gymnasium.

At the opposite end of the games room from the iron staircase, across from the gymnasium is a library containing books lent out for a fortnightly term.

Across the games room from the library, past the sweet shop, is a passage leading to the baths and toilets.

At the foot of the spiral staircase in the games room is the door beyond which steps lead down to the basement reading room (converted into a chapel in 1948).

Following the passage next to the Captain's office, a right turn leads to stone flight of steps giving access to the craft workshop and the band room. Beyond this flight of steps is the door to the Old Boys' Room.

The band room is accessed at the second landing of the stone flight of steps. The room is as arranged for Sunday morning Bible class.

The passage giving access to the Old Boys' room and band room also leads to the classroom.

The Dakeyne Farm

A leap into a brave new world.

In 1908, two boys approached Oliver Hind to discuss their interest in beginning a fresh life in Canada. He encouraged them in their plans and assisted in organising their outfitting and voyage and in finding them employment in farming when they arrived.

Contact was maintained through written correspondence and, over the following years, other boys whose interest was captivated by the accounts of their friends followed their course.

By 1911, 12 boys had crossed the Ocean to establish a new life in a new land and Oliver decided to see for himself how they fared.

When he arrived, he was delighted by the unspoilt nature of the place and what the boys had achieved. For one who was willing to learn and apply himself, there seemed great scope for advancement. After a few years of industry and thrift, a young man could raise enough capital to invest in his own farm. Compared with the prospects for a boy in Nottinghamshire those of a boy entering and growing with a developing nation appeared excellent.

The possibilities fired Oliver's imagination and he made enquiries to find a suitable farm which he would purchase to provide immigrating boys with an initial training that would enable them to obtain positions on Canadian farms and integrate smoothly into the community.

As news of his plans became known through his enquiries, he was offered free gifts of one square mile in the provinces of Alberta, Saskatchewan and Manitoba and exemption from taxes in Ontario to set up his farm in those territories; all seemingly eager to welcome hard working boys into their province.

The following year, Oliver made a second Atlantic crossing, this time accompanied by two agricultural experts with the purpose of inspecting various locations for a training farm.

After much consideration and discussion, he was persuaded by Colonel W. E. Thompson to select a site in the Windsor district of the province of Nova Scotia. The farm was purchased in 1913, the cost being shared between Oliver Hind and John Dane Player (fellow philanthropist and director of the Imperial Tobacco Company). It was named the Dakeyne Farm and consisted of 270 acres situated a short distance from the port of Falmouth and the town of Windsor. Apple orchards accounted for about 30 acres. The latest agricultural equipment was installed and a farm manager was employed to supervise and oversee the work carried out. Beyond this, the boys were left under their own control.

An average of 15 boys entered the scheme every year. The cost of emigrating was £15. If this was borne by the Club, the boy repaid it within two years of his employment in Canada. All other costs relating to a boy's accommodation and training were met by the Club. They were taught apple picking, horse grooming, ploughing and corn grinding by tractor, milking and general dairy work, dealing with cattle, calves and pigs, and farm maintenance. After completing a year on the farm, they were found suitable employment elsewhere in Canada.

Over the following years Oliver Hind sent new farming equipment and consignments of animals to stock the farm. In October 1916, his second despatch of animals included five red poll heifers and a large white boar and a sow. In 1923, he added a further 130 acres by purchasing an adjacent farm.

The Dakeyne Farm in Nova Scotia.

The Barn.

Boys setting off on their trans-Atlantic adventure are seen off by the company chaplain, Oliver Hind, and Alfred Davidson.

Boys settled in and starting a new life on the farm.

Darkness Falls

Theirs not to reason why,
Theirs but to do and die.

Early in 1914, Oliver Hind was entertained to a dinner by members of the Old Boys' Association. He perceived it a measure of success for the boys who had passed through the Club and was delighted by the way the occasion was organised and the exemplary behaviour of the young men attending. But storm clouds were looming.

May brought tidings of the death of The Boys' Brigade founder, Sir William Alexander Smith. Three months later, Europe was convulsed by the outbreak of the First World War.

The reason why the assassination of an Austrian Archduke in Serbia should spark a bitter conflict between the most powerful nations of Europe, three of which had heads of state who were cousins, might have appeared incomprehensible to those called upon to fight, but hundreds of thousands of young men saw it as their duty to protect their families from foreign aggressors and answered the call to defend their country.

Those Officers left behind because of their age or the importance placed upon their work strove to continue Boys' Brigade activities, but most had to be suspended for lack of Officers to organize them. Boys' Brigade Gazettes became dominated by lists of Officers and old boys who had won honours or lost their life in battle.

Proud of their courage but fearing for their safety, Oliver Hind maintained correspondence with two hundred and fifty three old boys fighting for their country. He had first-hand accounts of the dangerous and dire conditions they endured from members of his own family fighting at Gallipoli and Flanders.

Between 1914 and 1918, four hundred and fifty old boys of the Dakeyne Street Lads' Club offered their lives in the service of their country. Seventy three died. Many returned with disabling physical or mental injuries. Out of twelve who joined the Robin Hood Battalion, the only survivor was twice wounded.

Like other countries of the Empire who rallied to the British cause, Canada suffered many casualties. Of the boys who had migrated to start a new life farming there, at least five were killed fighting for the Canadian Army.

The Hind household had its share of misery brought by dreaded telegram. Oliver's younger brother, Lieutenant-Colonel Lawrence Arthur Hind, commander of the 1/7th (Territorial) Battalion of the Sherwood Foresters was killed together with thousands of others on the first day of the battle of the Somme, the 1st of July 1916. His body was never identified.

Lieutenant Jesse Francis Montague Hind, the only child of Oliver's elder brother, Jesse William, was killed in action on the 27th September in the same campaign aged 23.

News arrived that a cousin, Oliver Ashover Hind, who had emigrated to Australia in 1910, was killed in Israel on the 3rd of November 1917, a trooper in the 1st Australian Light Horse Regiment.

Devastated by the loss of his only child, Jesse William Hind equipped an Orthopaedic Hospital at Trent Bridge to treat disabled soldiers. Named the Monty Ward in memory of his son, it provided pioneering treatment for injured soldiers and was acknowledged to be the best hospital of its kind in the country, ameliorating or curing hundreds of men who would otherwise have been crippled for life. He became Chairman of the Voluntary Aid Detachment (VAD) Hospital in West Bridgford where he administered an expansion from ninety to a hundred and fifty beds, for which he was awarded the certificate of the British Red Cross Society. In 1934, he was knighted for his service in support of injured soldiers and his contribution to the Midland Eye Infirmary and Harlow Wood Orthopaedic Hospital.

After the war, a memorial, designed by the Nottingham architect Harry Gill, containing the name of seventy three old boys and the relatives of Oliver Hind who had been killed in the war, was set in a prominent position in the Dakeyne Street Club. From 1918, an armistice service, culminating in a single bugle-call last post, was a significant event of every year for the 2nd Nottingham Company of The Boys' Brigade.

Jesse William Hind purchased a farm outside of the village of Kinoulton for the purpose of training ex-service men in agriculture. He changed its name from Pasture Hall to Vimy Ridge Farm and planted 184 poplar trees, similar to those that lined avenues of northern France, along the lane leading to the farmhouse. There was one tree for each of the 9th Battalion of the Sherwood Foresters' soldiers, including his son, who had lost his life at the battle of the Somme.

The 1914 - 1918 War Memorial.

Dakeyne Street Lads' Club old boys lost in the conflict.

E. Anderson	J. George	H. Lee	F. Robinson
W. A. Burton	F. Hudson	A. F. Mantle	O. Smith
C. Baker	G. M. Higgs	A. Mitchell	P. Smith
S. E. Clark	R. Hardy	J. Musson	A. Shepherd
E. Clark	G. Hodson	W. Marshall	J. H. Sanders
R. Clarke	P. Hutchinson	H. Murfet	A. Swain
C. Colgrave	H. Hodges	W. Murphy	J. Spinks
G. Cook	G. Hill	J. McGreavy	W. L. Savidge
W. G. Cooke	H. C. Hammond	B. McGreavy	G. Spencer
E. Carter	H. Hampson	J. W. Marriott	S. Stones
C. Christmas	M. Hallam	H. Parkes	G. Sharpe
F. Daniels	W. Hallam	P. Parkes	A. Snowden
A. G. Elliott	H. Hurt	W. J. Parker	F. Tomlinson
H. Frost	A. Harrison	G. Prior	A. E. Wilson
E. Greenberry	H. Ickes	H. Russell	G. Williams
N. G. Guy	A. Keward	Russell-Horace	W. Whitehead
A. Gent	E. King	W. J. Roberts	G. W. Else
A. Cumberpatch	R. W. Hamilton	W. Soles	C. W. Newman

Lest We Forget

The Dakeyne Street Lads' Club (After the Storm)

Picking up the pieces.

The war had taken a deadly toll. Many children had lost their father. Others had returned so physically or mentally mutilated as to be unfit for work. Traumatised soldiers cowered in corners and under beds or patrolled the streets as if on sentry duty.

Industries that had been diverted to war production had to readjust to civilian goods at a time when there was little money to spare for purchases. Jobs had been filled while soldiers were away. Where this was by women, the women were displaced by the returning men and lost their income. Large numbers of unemployed competed for scant work.

In this harsh environment, in addition to revitalising pre-war activities, a popular Christmas event was introduced into the Dakeyne Street Lads' Club calendar. A free Christmas morning breakfast was provided for five to six hundred young children selected from the most desperately poor families in the area.

Large provisions of food to more than fully satisfy the appetites of these hundreds of hungry children were brought in, under the supervision of the Company Quartermaster (at first George Guy and later George Arthur Spick), who carried out a similar function for other major events and at the annual camp.

From six-o-clock in the morning, Officers, friends, and senior boys arrived at the Club to make preparations. The breakfast was cooked. Tables and seating were arranged in the drill hall. The boys were despatched with a list of names and addresses to collect the children (a bitter-sweet assignment as some small faces pressed anxiously against window panes were not included in the list).

The breakfast commenced between eight-thirty and nine and after the children had consumed as much as they could they were supplied with paper bags to take what remained home; no doubt to be shared with other members of their family. Finally, they were given a small gift from Santa's sack. For some it may have been their only present.

It was an exhausting but deeply rewarding experience for the Officers, boys, and helpers. Very much appreciated by all involved, it was continued until the outbreak of the Second World War.

After a lapse of four years, Boys' Brigade activities began to reassert themselves. The first post-war Nottingham Battalion demonstration was staged at the Nottingham Albert Hall in 1919 and the guest of honour was Douglas, the younger son of Sir William Alexander Smith.

In March 1920, Oliver Hind was invited as guest of honour at a dinner and presentation arranged by the Dakeyne Street Old Boys' Association. The occasion was attended by one hundred and twenty old boys and guests including the Lord Mayor, Lady Mayoress, and Sheriff of Nottingham, Richard Swain, John Auger Dixon, John Player, Captain H. A. Brown, and members of Oliver's family. After dinner, the guest of honour was presented with a portrait of himself painted by Noel Denholm Davis, which was unveiled in the old boys' room by the Lady Mayoress. George Guy, speaking for the old boys, said the gift represented an emblem of the gratitude, esteem, and love felt by them for their revered Captain.

In his speech of thanks, Oliver Hind expressed his pride and respect for the old boys who had nearly all fought in the war. He transferred the portrait to his home at Edwalton Hall and ordered a copy to be painted by the same artist. This was hung in the Club games room above the war memorial.

Boys continued to migrate to Canada and Oliver Hind visited regularly to assess the success of the venture and meet any deficiencies in land or equipment. In 1921 he made the crossing accompanied by Alfred Eric Davidson who was sixteen years of age. Son of Alfred Davidson, the Club Superintendent, Alfred Eric was the latest recruit for the farm. He made a holiday visit home a year later but returned to build a life in Canada.

On the 8th of September 1921 there was a momentous ceremony at Nottingham Castle at which Air-Marshall Sir Hugh Trenchard, K.C.B., D.S.O unveiled a statue commemorating ace fighter pilot Albert Ball, who had been killed in action on the 7th of May 1917, at the age of twenty. Born in Lenton, Albert had been a been a highly courageous pilot and a national hero. The ceremony attracted large crowds and included a spectacular air display. As a measure of their level of distinction, the Dakeyne Street Lads' Club band, under the leadership of Albert Pounder, was invited to form part of this prestigious occasion by playing in the Nottingham Market Square from 2.30 to 3.30pm.

The war years had been as damaging for the Hind family as any other. Oliver's younger brother and partner in the family firm, Lawrence Arthur, had been killed. Shortly after the war, his father, who was the senior partner in the firm and Oliver's mentor, also died. So far, Oliver had invested in the region of £27,000 setting up and maintaining the Dakeyne Street Lads' Club and the Dakeyne Farm. Now in his late forties and denied the support of his father and brother, it was clear to him that he would not be able to sustain this level of expense indefinitely. With a view to securing the long-term viability of the two ventures, he began to consider ways in which the Club and Farm might become more self-supporting.

Since the Dakeyne Street Lads' Club had started, about 2500 boys had enjoyed and benefited from the facilities that had been made available. Many had gained better employment as a result of the education and training they had received and the prestige attached to having passed through such a widely respected Club. Oliver Hind felt the time had come for some of these boys to demonstrate their appreciation for what had been done for them. By turning a small portion of the financial advantage they had gained to the Club's use, they could help to enable further generations to benefit from what the Club had to offer.

During the annual meeting of the Old Boys' Association in 1921, he made an appeal for help towards meeting the running costs of the Club. He pointed out that the average annual expense amounted to £1,500 and that, because of unusual repairs and alterations that had been carried out, expenses for the previous year had amounted to £3,400 of which £1,331 was still outstanding. The Old Boys' Association agreed by vote to submit to the use of the Club £50 from their fund of £80. A relatively small, but no doubt welcome contribution.

Cinema had arrived and a Saturday night showing in the Club gymnasium became a popular addition to the weekly entertainment. Forthcoming titles, film stars, and number-of-reels were advertised in advance. Being a non-Club night, attendance was open to the general public. In February 1922, to acknowledge his twenty first year of service in The Boys' Brigade, Oliver Hind entertained the membership of the Club to tea followed by a film show.

The following year, Alfred Davidson made an announcement that took his fellow Officers by surprise. Their Captain, Oliver Hind, now approaching his fiftieth year of bachelorhood, was to marry. When quizzed as to who was the bride to be, Alfred informed them proudly that it was none other than his own eldest daughter, Mary, who worked as a nurse at the City Hospital.

The wedding took place in London on the 31st of July 1924 and on their return from honeymoon a reception was given by three hundred and fifty boys at the Dakeyne Street Lads' Club. Wedding gifts included an electric lamp and an autograph book containing the boys' signatures. Later, the couple were presented with an antique music case by George Guy on behalf of the Old Boys' Association and a large silver tray by Richard Swain on behalf of the Officers of the Battalion.

In July 1925, Oliver set out again on the now familiar trans-Atlantic crossing, this time accompanied by his new wife. As well as showing her the beautiful location and satisfying himself that all was proceeding well, he was keen to find a way to put the Farm on a long-term secure financial footing.

While registered at a hotel in Halifax, he received a request from Mr. Edgar Nelson Rhodes, who was also staying at the hotel, to meet him and discuss the principle and the operation of the Farm. Happy to oblige, he accepted the invitation and, after the conversation had been in progress for some time, he realised he was talking to the recently appointed Prime Minister of Nova Scotia. The Premier indicated a considerable interest in the purpose of the Farm, but, since he had not yet had time to order his Government, asked Oliver to bear with him until a future visit, when some arrangement would be devised that would release him of the financial burden. It was a step in the right direction.

The following year, 1926, was notable for two anniversaries.

On the 31st of January, Oliver Hind celebrated a quarter of a century of service to The Boys' Brigade at a tea arranged at the Dakeyne Street Lads' Club. He was presented with a mahogany timepiece by the boys of the Company and a mahogany writing desk by Richard Swain, the Battalion President, on behalf of Officers of the Battalion. Both gifts contained inscriptions testifying to the esteem and affection in which he was regarded.

On the final Saturday of October, Alfred Davidson treated the boys of the Club to a tea and cinema show in celebration of his twenty one years with The Boys' Brigade.

Having joined as second in command when Oliver Hind first took over the Captaincy of the 2nd Nottingham Company, Alfred had assiduously fulfilled the functions of Superintendent of the Dakeyne Street Lads' Club since the beginning. Both he and his wife, Alice Margaret, had devoted a considerable portion of their lives to carefully managing and organising the Club activities and were greatly revered by the boys. Among many other tasks, Alice ran a sweet shop at the end of the games room and organised the Monday afternoon mothers' meeting. She also looked after the bank where boys deposited money to pay the cost and accumulate a fund of pocket money for the annual camp. This arrangement was extended to provide a general banking service where boys were encouraged to be thrifty by being offered a 5% interest rate on balances over 10 shillings.

As well as caring for six children of their own, Alfred and Alice accepted responsibility for the guardianship of two orphan boys. On one occasion, a waif of a child had been found stranded and in a miserable condition in the Midland Railway Station. He had no home, his father was dead and his mother was dying. Alfred and Alice took him into their home and looked after him. When old enough, he emigrated to Canada where, by 1926, he owned a farm and was married with a family of six children.

Alfred and Alice were presented with gold watches as a mark of love and appreciation of the Officers and boys for their faithful and unstinting service.

In 1927, an arrangement was finally agreed upon with regard to the long-term security of the Dakeyne Farm. The operating costs were transferred to the

Government of Nova Scotia who were left with an option to purchase the land after five years if the revised scheme proved successful. The operation was expanded to attract boys from all over England and the number of immigrants increased. Arthur Smith, an old boy of the Dakeyne Street Lads' Club who had emigrated to Canada as part of the scheme, was retained as Farm Manager.

Oliver Hind, whose health was deteriorating, was pleased and relieved by the ultimate outcome of his negotiations. Not only did it remove the weight of an ongoing financial responsibility from his shoulders but the new scheme was designed to provide opportunity for a greater number of boys. He travelled to the Farm for the last time in June 1928 and the following year he and John Player, his partner in the venture, conferred ownership of the Dakeyne Farm to the National Association of Boys' Clubs. Since the outset, a hundred and fifty boys had migrated from Nottingham to the Dakeyne Farm and had settled to a new life in Canada.

In June 1927, the Dakeyne Street Lads' Club were sent a flag by Marriott C. Morris on behalf of the Germantown Boys' Club, which he had founded in Philadelphia, USA. It resulted from visit he had made to Dakeyne Street three years earlier and was presented to the Club by the Executive Secretary of the International Boys' Club Federation, Mr C. J. Atkinson.

The annual camp had been held at various sites around the country. In 1924 the Club were given permission to camp in the grounds of Wrea Head, a farm owned by Mrs. Ellis, widow of a previous MP for Rushcliffe, at Scalby near Scarborough (the stay included a visit to the warship H.M.S. Royal Oak); in 1925, the Company had formed part of a combined camp at Yarmouth; in 1928, the Company camped at Rhyl in North Wales; in 1929, the Company visited Mablethorpe.

Towards the close of the 1920's, the Company received an unexpected inheritance from a Mr. Naylor, a retired gentleman who had once been a fish and chip shop owner in Sneinton. While having no known connection with the Club, he demonstrated his goodwill by asking Oliver Hind to call on him at his place of retirement in West Bridgford in order to discuss a proposed bequest. The legacy was used to acquire land on the east coast that would provide a permanent site for Company camps.

After examining various locations, it was decided to purchase a field on the southern edge of the village of Chapel St. Leonards on the Lincolnshire coast. From the summer of 1930 onwards, this was the setting for many happy and successful summer camps.

The team of officers at the time of Oliver Hind's wedding in 1924.

Front row: Claud Whitaker, Alfred Davidson, Oliver Hind, George Guy, and Glen Fisher. Second row: Harry Green, Charles Sansom, William Gant, John Stokes, Harry Shaw, and George Spick. Back row: Claud Harris and Albert Pounder.

The Company in 1920.

The Band in 1920 under the direction of Albert Pounder.

9

SYLLABUS.

Sunday.
Bible Class 11.15

Monday.
Company Drill ... ...7.30 to 8.20 Mr. Stokes and
Mr Fisher
,, ,, ...8.30 to 9.20 ...Mr. Spick and
Mr. Sansom
Band (Recruits) ... ...8.0 to 9.30 ...Mr. Pounder

Tuesday.
Wireless ... ...7.0 to 8.0 ...Mr. Pinder.
Physical Training ... ...7.30 to 8.30 ...Mr. Martin
,, ,, ...8.30 to 9.30 ...Mr. Martin
Ambulance (Junior) ...7.30 to 8.30 ...Staff-Sgt. Hopewell
English Composition ...7.30 to 8.30 ...Mr. Hearn
Arithmetic ... ...8.30 to 9.30 ...Mr. King
Shorthand ... ...8.30 to 9.30 ...Mr. Harris

Wednesday.
Recruits Drill ... ...7.15 to 8.15 ...Mr. Shaw
Gymnastics (Senior) ...7.30 to 8.30 ...Mr. Swift
Band ... ...8.0 to 9.30 ...Mr. Pounder

Thursday.
Recruits Drill ... ...7.15 to 8.15 ...Mr. Harris.
Ambulance (Senior) ...7.30 to 8.30 ...Mr. Guy
Handwork ... ...7.30 to 8.30 ...Mr. Lowe
,, ...8.30 to 9.30 ...Mr. Lowe
Shorthand (Juniors) ...7.30 to 9.0 ...Mr. Horney
,, (Seniors) ...8.30 to 9.30 ...Mr. Harris

Friday.
Signalling ... ...7.30 to 8.30 ...Mr. Barton
Gymnastics (Juniors) ...7.30 to 8.15 ...Mr. Swift
,, (Juniors) ...8.15 to 9.0 ...Mr. Swift
Special Physical Training 8.0 to 9.0 ...Mr. Shaw and
Mr. Green
Draughts Class ... ...8.30 to 9.30 ...Mr. Barton
Saturday.—Athletic Ground open at 2 p.m.—Football Matches.
Cinema and free night, 6.45 to 9.30.

The session programme for 1922.

44

Christmas breakfast in the drill hall.

Summer recreation at the Trent Lane Sports Ground River Bank.

Camp at Mablethorpe in the summer of 1929.

Sergeant G. Hopewell, Sergeant J. Terry, Lance-Corporal W. Garner, Corporal T. Hopewell, and Sergeant T. Hazard receive the King's medal, the most prestigious of all Boys' Brigade awards, in 1929.

Throughout the 1920's, the Dakeyne Street Lads' Club performed well in sport (both the boys' and old boys' teams featured regularly in the sport pages of the Nottingham Evening Post), gymnastics (the team featured several times at the Albert Hall in London), music (the forty piece silver band had featured at numerous significant civic events), and inter-Company drill and sporting competitions. These successes culminated in 1929, when five boys (Sergeants G. Hopewell, J. Terry, T. Hazard, Corporal T. Hopewell, and Lance-Corporal W. Garner) broke the record for a single Company in The Boys' Brigade by all achieving the Brigade's highest award, the King's Badge, in a single session.

The End of an Era

Many lads will thank God through their tears for what he was to them.

Oliver and Mary Hind were graced with three daughters; Audrey born early 1925, Olive late 1926, and Margaret early 1929. But their domestic bliss was tarnished by concerns over Oliver's declining health. During the latter part of the 1920's he was increasingly troubled by a heart complaint.

There were improvements and relapses. At the Old Boys' Association annual meeting in March 1927, he was congratulated by the President of the Association, William Skellett, upon his restoration to health. The following year he was not fit to attend the meeting and his honoured place was taken by Alfred Davidson.

The period since the First World War had been one of slowly improving living standards in most working class homes; houses in the Sneinton area were connected with a supply of electricity from 1926 and home entertainment was provided through the medium of radio. But the economic system of the western world was thrown into chaos by the Wall Street Stock Market Crash of October 1929. Important financial institutions floundered; vast sums were wiped from share prices; thousands were made bankrupt; it triggered the start of the great depression.

Against a backdrop of failing health and financial uncertainty, Oliver Hind had to consider the future well-being of his young family as well as the long term sustainability of the Dakeyne Street Lads' Club. His wife, an experienced nurse, would see these concerns only exacerbating the danger of his condition.

Early in 1930, they took a voyage to South Africa in the hope that the change of climate and relaxation would prove favourable to his health but when welcomed home by the boys at Dakeyne Street in April, he still appeared far from well.

During the first weekend of the next month, the Company contributed a pyramid display at the annual demonstration of The Boys' Brigade at the Royal Albert Hall in London. Dressed in Pierrot costumes the team entertained the audience by constructing fourteen difficult human pyramids. It was an act that was repeated the following week on King Edward Park in front of thousands of spectators, for the benefit of parents and friends.

On the 4th of July, Private George C. Bradshaw of the 2nd Nottingham Company of The Boys' Brigade helped save a young woman who had thrown herself into the River Trent. In recognition of his bravery, the following October the 7th the Lord Mayor of Nottingham presented him with The Boys' Brigade Cross of Valour. He was fifteen years of age.

During the summer of 1930, Alfred Davidson retired from his long-standing position as Superintendent of the Dakeyne Street Lads' Club because of declining health. He continued to serve Nottingham in his capacity of City Junior Probation Officer.

Having lost his highly-valued Superintendent and seeking means to resolve the issue of the long-term viability of the Club, Oliver Hind approached the Education Committee with a proposal that would relinquish him and his family from being the soul providers of finance and would provide a replacement for Alfred Davidson.

An agreement was concluded whereby the property of the Club, with the exception of the Chapel St. Leonards camp ground, was to transfer from Oliver Hind to the charge of the Education Committee who would undertake to satisfy the debts incurred in running the Club.

The Club was placed under the direction of a governing body consisting of nine members, three to represent the Education Committee and six to represent the interests of the Club and The Boys' Brigade. The Dakeyne Street Evening Continuation School was to operate as before under the control of the Education Committee and further use was to be made of Club premises during the day by running a special school for unemployed juveniles between the ages of thirteen and twenty one. A full time Warden was to be employed by the Education Committee to take over the responsibilities of the retired Superintendent.

The changes, necessary as they were to secure the future of the Club, created consternation amongst some of the Officers and old boys who feared the nature of the Club was about to change. At a meeting of the Old Boys' Association in October 1930, Oliver Hind explained that the new arrangement would leave the activities of the Club unaffected and that he would remain their Captain.

Unfortunately, his illness prevented him from spending much time at Dakeyne Street. Having written a message to the boys in a DAKO Magazine which was launched by the new Warden in November, he spent several months convalescing at a house purchased in Skegness. He died at his residence at Edwalton Hall on the 7th of July 1931 at the age of fifty-eight.

Hundreds of people, including a parade of two hundred boys and a hundred old boys from the Dakeyne Street Lads' Club, attended his funeral service at the Church of the Holy Rood at Edwalton to pay their last respects. The Church was too small to accommodate the numbers.

Simultaneously, a memorial service took place at St. Mary's Church in the Lace Market, Nottingham, where hundreds more colleagues and friends from all spheres of his life came to show their affection and admiration. It was stated in the address that, "many lads will thank God through their tears for what he was to them".

Beyond his work at the Dakeyne Street Lads' Club, in 1911 Oliver Hind was appointed a Justice of the Peace and fulfilled his duties in this capacity by sitting usually in the Juvenile Court. He was a member of the Government's Advisory Committee on Probation and of the Juvenile Organisation Committee for both the country and the city. He served on the Notts Playing Fields Association. He had been elected to be President of the Nottingham Incorporated Law Society in February 1931. He was about to be appointed Vice-President of The National Association of Boys' Clubs. As a solicitor, he had been a partner in the firm Wells and Hind for the whole of his career and in the sphere of business was a director of the Sherwood Colliery Co., the Nottingham Patent Brick Co. and Secretary for the Notts and Erewash Valley Colliery Owners' Association.

His death marked the end of an era for the 2nd Nottingham Company of The Boys' Brigade. Mary Hind succeeded her husband as Chairman of the Governing Body and the name of the Club was changed from the Dakeyne Street Lads' Club to the Oliver Hind Boys' Club.

Two years later, on the 23rd of July 1933, Mary Hind's father, Alfred Davidson, collapsed and died at his home of retirement in Bottesford during a visit of boys from the Club. His contribution as Superintendent of the Dakeyne Street Lads' Club had been outstanding and for many years he had coupled this with the responsibilities of City Juvenile Probation Officer for Nottingham. If persuaded it would be of benefit, he occasionally recommended a term with The Boys' Brigade as a means of improving the behaviour of a youthful offender. This role was taken over by Jack R. Bickerdike, who, with fellow Boys' Brigade Officers George Spick, Harry Shaw and Albert Ball, led thirty boys from the 2nd Nottingham Company at the head of Alfred's funeral procession at Bottesford.

The tragedy of Alfred's sudden death was compounded when thirteen-year-old boy, James Flanders, was drowned in the River Trent, having gone for a swim with friends on returning from the funeral.

The Oliver Hind Boys' Club

Highs and lows.

The newly constituted Governing Body appointed Richard Frederick Millard to be the first full-time paid Warden for the Club. He took up the appointment in October 1930, initially for a fixed three year term.

Richard was born in Cumberland in late 1897 where his father was a Church of England clergyman. In the First World War he had been the youngest army Officer sent to Gallipoli and later served in Palestine and France. He was twice wounded. After the war he became Warden of Shrewsbury School Mission and Boys' Club in Liverpool and later was appointed the first Secretary of the National Association of Boys' Clubs (the object of which was to promote the development of boys and young men in achieving their full physical, intellectual, social and spiritual potential through a network of clubs). The National Association of Boys' Clubs had taken responsibility for managing the Dakeyne Farm and, as part of his work, Richard travelled to Canada to examine the process of juvenile emigration. While there, he took the opportunity to travel and study various boys' clubs in the United States.

His term of office as Warden included a visit to Dakeyne Street by His Royal Highness Prince Henry, the Duke of Gloucester, son of King George V and President of the National Association of Boys' Clubs.

On the evening of the 25th of February 1932, spectators lined the streets to cheer the Duke's passing car and at 8pm he was greeted at the Club by members of Oliver Hind's family, the Governing Body, the Warden, and the Director of Education, the Chief Constable, the Lord Major and Lady Mayoress, and the Sheriff of Nottingham.

He was given a guided tour of the premises during which boys attempted to appear engrossed in normal activities. They played table-tennis, billiards, and snooker in the main games room, bound volunteers in arm slings and splints in a first-aid class, read quietly in the library, demonstrated their craftsmanship in the workshop, practiced shorthand, sparred in a boxing ring under the tutelage of off-duty volunteer policemen, and played cards and drafts. The tour took an hour and at the end the Prince signed the visitors book before standing silently and respectfully before the names of the fallen listed on the war memorial. Before leaving, he told Mary Hind that he had thoroughly enjoyed the evening.

As he left, the band played the National Anthem and the Club members, mysteriously assembled between the Club entrance and gates, raised four lusty cheers. Bravo!

In January 1933, the Officers of the Club were invited to a special celebration at the Boot's Cafe on Pelham Street in central Nottingham to commemorate the twenty fifth anniversary of the opening of the Dakeyne Street Lads' Club. After being treated to a supper, they were awarded gifts by the Lord Mayor as a token of thanks for their youth work in the city.

At the end of March, a 'Pageant of Boyhood Through the Ages' was staged at the Club on two consecutive nights to commemorate its successes over the previous twenty five years.

But cracks were beginning to show with the new administrative structure. The Education Committee which employed the Warden was bureaucratic and secular in perspective. The Boys' Brigade Officers were steeped in the tradition of the Club which was built upon pillars of religion and discipline; they gave freely of their time and their relationship with the boys was based upon friendship and trust. While the Education Committee teachers commanded respect, the Boys' Brigade Officers also commanded admiration and loyalty amongst the boys in their charge.

It was a task of the Warden to reconcile these conflicting perspectives and in this respect, Richard Millard, whose background was in administration in a secular setting, was a problematic choice. Trying to implement certain changes of procedure, he clashed with the Officers and created a disharmony that resulted in a decline in the number of boys taking part in activities. In the summer of 1933, only 43 boys attended the annual camp.

Richard Millard resigned in the October and terminated his term of office on the 31st of December 1933. Mr. O. H. Newbery, previously an assistant master at the Claremont Senior Boys' School, took over as Headmaster of the Junior Instruction Centre at Dakeyne Street on the 8th of January, 1934. A new arrangement was set up whereby the management of the Trust was put under the control of the Governing Body and the role of the Education Committee was reduced to managing the Junior Instruction Centre, paying a yearly amount to cover rent and fuel, lighting, and cleaning costs.

Between the time of Richard Millard's leaving and the appointment of another full-time Warden, the duties of Captain were taken over by Claud Harris. A close associate of the Hind family who worked in the offices of Wells and Hind, Claud had been an Officer in the 2nd Nottingham Company for many years and was a Trustee on the Governing Body.

The Chapel St Leonards Camp Site.

Preparing for a comfortable night's sleep on a straw filled palliasse.

Tent inspection.

Orderlies for the day peeling potatoes to feed two hundred.

The Arthur Stevenson Years

Second to none.

The Hind family at Chapel St Leonards in the summer of 1933.

Regimental Sergeant-Major Arthur Stevenson was due to retire from the 1st Battalion of the Sherwood Foresters in the Spring of 1934. Born in Newark in the summer of 1890, he enlisted in the army at the age of seventeen and during the course of his military career had been a notable athlete and army fencing champion. Having fought and suffered injuries in the First World War, he had taken a position as Instruction Officer at the Army School of Physical Training.

His Colonel was acquainted with members of the Governing Body of the Oliver Hind Boys' Club and believed he saw in Arthur characteristics that would make him ideally suited to the post of Warden. He spoke to Arthur about the vacancy and, meeting with an enthusiastic response, recommended him to the Trustees. Arthur was interviewed by the Officers of the Club at Edwalton Hall and was offered and accepted the position of Warden, starting at the end of the season.

The King's birthday honours list published on the 4th of June 1934 awarded Arthur an M.B.E. for his services to the army (the same list conferred a knighthood upon Jesse William Hind for his contribution to the treatment of injured soldiers during and after the First World War). As a measure of his eagerness to take over his new responsibilities, Arthur attended the Chapel St. Leonards camp soon after receiving his M.B.E. award.

His manner was authoritative but approachable and friendly. One of the characteristics recognised by his Colonel that favoured his appointment and which was soon to establish his personality as a dominant influence in the Club was his talent for commanding a high standard of discipline by gaining the confidence and developing the respect and affection of those under his charge. He had an acute memory for details and, by displaying a genuine interest in the life of every boy, made each feel a sense of belonging and attachment to the Club. If rules were transgressed, he would rigorously enforce discipline, but once an offence had been atoned for, the incident was at an end. By acting judiciously, showing no discrimination in his treatment of boys, and promoting a sense of esprit-de-corps and loyalty to the Club, he raised the 2nd Company once again to the forefront of the Nottingham Battalion.

Once settled in his new role, he began to introduce new ideas, many stemming from his experiences in the army and all designed to strengthen the cohesion of the Club membership. One popular innovation, recalling his former army-champion days, was a fencing class.

He also introduced the 'March Weekend' where NCOs from other parts of the country were invited to visit the 2nd Nottingham Company. Meals were prepared and served at Dakeyne Street and the guests were supplied with bedding and blankets and provided with a room in which to sleep. On the Sunday morning, they emerged from the confusion at the Club to form up in uniform and take part in the annual Battalion Parade to the Albert Hall. Friendships were formed and the weekend was enjoyed by both the guests and their hosts.

Strengthening the unity of the Company being central to his approach, the annual camp provided the new Captain with a wonderful opportunity to build a family spirit by drawing everyone into activities and leaving no one without a place in the camp society.

One regular feature was a football match organised between teams representing Freddie Farrow and Cyril Whiteley, two old boys who, though unable to play a full active part, derived considerable pleasure from their involvement in camp life. The game invariably ended in a draw with Freddie's eleven scoring an equalizer in the final seconds.

It often happened that Arthur Stevenson's birthday coincided with the camp week. Whenever it did, he celebrated the occasion by entertaining the boys to a party and fireworks.

Under Arthur Stevenson's stewardship, the Club recovered from its fall in membership (eighty additional members joining in the new Captain's first year) and regained its standing in team sports, gymnastic displays, and Battalion competitions.

Encouraged by Mary Hind, the Old Boys' Association, which had languished during the Richard Millard's time as Warden, also became reinvigorated under the Presidency of William Betts (the Betts brothers William, Ernest, Archie and Frank were stalwart members of the Old Boys' football team which featured weekly in the sports section of the Nottingham Evening Post).

Bandmaster Albert Pounder, who had been taken ill in the autumn of 1935, died in January 1936 at the age of seventy nine.

Albert's life had been devoted to music. Even in his employment, which was in the manufacture of leather goods, he specialised in making musical instrument cases.

As a child, he had saved his pocket money, bought a flute, and joined a fife and drum band. His enthusiasm and natural talent was recognised by band leader Arthur Hindley who encouraged him to learn the cornet and become a member of his popular 'Sax Tuba Band'. Albert became a proficient instrumentalist and, from 1880, gained second place in three consecutive years at a national contest for solo cornet staged at Crystal Palace in London.

From the age of eighteen, he took charge of several bands (at one time he was simultaneously the Bandmaster of five local bands) and in 1886 became Band-Sergeant in the Robin Hood Battalion of the Sherwood Forester Regiment where Arthur Hindley was the Bandmaster. Taking over the senior position when Arthur became ill, Albert was Bandmaster of the Robin Hood Battalion until the outbreak of the First World War.

He also involved himself with the Nottingham Battalion of The Boys' Brigade from the outset and was Bandmaster at the Dakeyne Street Lads' Club since its opening. At The Boys' Brigade Jubilee Celebration staged at Notts County Football Ground in the summer of 1933, he was presented with a gift to commemorate his forty-four years of service to the Battalion.

At the time of his illness, he was Bandmaster of the 2nd and 1st Nottingham Companies of The Boys Brigade and of the Nottingham Boys' High School Officers' Training Corp Band.

He had a widespread reputation as Bandmaster of outstanding ability and, under his leadership, the level of performance of the Oliver Hind Boys' Club Band was held in the highest regard. It was a standard that was to be sustained by fellow musician and Boys' Brigade Officer, Leslie Hutchby.

With an ex-Regimental Sergeant Major at the helm, the 2nd Company was well placed to compete on the parade ground. In 1936, it won the Battalion drill competition with Colour-Sergeant Frank Betts securing the Sergeant's Championship. The following year, Sergeant Ernest Dykes was selected as one of three members to represent the Nottingham Battalion at the coronation of King George VI.

By 1939, under Arthur Stevenson's stewardship, the Club membership had risen again to almost three hundred boys. The Company fared well at sports, gymnastics, and music and continued to contribute popular items at the annual Battalion demonstrations staged at the Empire Theatre. On the first weekend of May in 1939, it entered an item in The Boys' Brigade annual demonstration at the Royal Albert Hall in London entitled, the 'Circus'. Arranged and directed by Jack Bickerdike, this consisted of various performances of boys simulating acts that would appear under a big top, including a unicycle.

The camp that year took place at Chapel St Leonards from August 4th to the 11th. On the following 1st of September, German forces attacked Poland. On the 3rd of September, Britain declared war upon Germany. Europe was once again enveloped in bloody turmoil. To the consternation of fathers who dreaded their sons being dragged into the same bitter mire that they had endured twenty five years before in what was claimed to be the war to end all wars, men above the age of eighteen were once again called up to defend their country. Younger men were recruited to take part in civil defence.

At first, every attempt was made to maintain activities at the Boys' Club. In May 1940, the band entertained the public to an open-air concert at Colwick Woods Park. But as the war intensified, in deference to the requirements of civil safety under the threat of bomber attacks, most classes were disbanded.

The outcome of the war was far from certain and it was a time of grave concern for families whose fathers, brothers, and sons had been sent into action. In May 1940, news arrived that Herbert Long, an old boy of the Club, was missing in France. His family and friends were relieved later when it was reported that he had been captured and was held prisoner. By June, many more families were nervously awaiting news as to whether their loved ones had been safely evacuated from the beaches of Dunkirk.

But this war was as dangerous for civilians as it was for the armed forces.

Volunteer senior boys from the Club were trained to take part in a messenger service that was to operate if there was a break in communications between strategic nerve centres in the locality. But even this project was brought to a close because of the danger of bombing raids.

On the night spanning the 8th and 9th of May 1941, a bombing raid in the area surrounding the Oliver Hind Boys' Club was particularly severe.

The air raid shelter situated in the basement of a building on Dakeyne Street suffered a direct hit. All twenty one who were seeking protection within its walls, including two boys from the Club and their families, were killed.

The old boys' room in the Club received the impact of an exploding bomb and a large painting stored there for protection, caught a piece of flying shrapnel.

The sitting room of the Warden's home also took a blast and was rendered uninhabitable. Arthur Stevenson and his wife were invited by Mary Hind to stay at Edwalton Hall while repairs took place. They were grateful to receive and gladly accepted the offer.

Two years and three months into the war in Europe, it escalated into a world-wide conflict with the Japanese invasion of British and United States protected territories in the east. In January 1942, Staff-Sergeant Alfred Munton, an old boy of the Club, was posted missing after the storming of Hong Kong.

In February, an army cadet unit was set up in the Club premises. It admitted boys between the ages of fourteen and seventeen years and was designed to prepare them for possible military action. The basement room was converted into a firing range and the sports ground at Trent Lane was used for military manoeuvres.

March brought news of the death in North Africa of twenty-one year old William Arthur Hopewell, a former member of the Oliver Hind Boys' Club and St. John Ambulance Brigade. He had been a Leading Aircraftman in the Royal Air Force Volunteer Reserve 70th Squadron. The following July it was reported that Private Frederick T. W. Taylor of the Army Dental Corp, a former Boys' Club member, was missing in action in the Middle East.

But by the middle of 1942, the danger of bombing raids had receded. At the end of August, the 2nd Nottingham Boys Brigade Company silver band and the drum and bugle band of the Civil Defence Cadet Corps played at a parade at the Nottingham Forest where 7000 teenagers from Nottingham youth clubs marched passed Sir Stafford Cripps, Lord Privy Seal and Leader of the House of Commons.

In September 1943 it was reported that driver John Smeeton of the Royal Army Service Corp, an old boy of the Oliver Hind Boys' Club, had been killed in action in the Middle East.

From the outset of war, shortage of food was a serious problem. Rationing was introduced limiting what could be purchased to an individual allowance based upon available supplies. Sweets became so scarce that there was little point in opening Oliver Hind Boys' Club sweet shop. To counter this and restore a little cheer as the end of the war drew near, Arthur Stevenson applied for grants to enable him to sell food and drink that could be prepared and served to boys at the Club. The Dakeyne Street Canteen opened in 1944.

December 1944 brought tidings of the death of RAF pilot Sergeant Charles Jackson, at twenty-one years of age. As a boy, he was the principal trombonist in the Oliver Hind Boys' Club Silver Band. He had gained his wings training in South Africa the previous February and lost his life flying for the Royal Air Force Volunteer Reserve 607 Squadron in Burma. He left a young wife, Doris Joan, and baby child.

At the end of the war, Arthur Stevenson resigned from his position as Warden of the Oliver Hind Boys' Club having completed eleven years of service. He became Secretary for the Nottingham Battalion until his retirement in 1955. He died in December 1967.

The Team of Officers during the Captaincy of Arthur Stevenson.

Front row: Albert Ball, Harry Shaw, Arthur Stevenson, George Spick, and Leslie Hutchby. Back row: Jack Bickerdike, Len Shepherd, Bill Whitley, and Harold Wright.

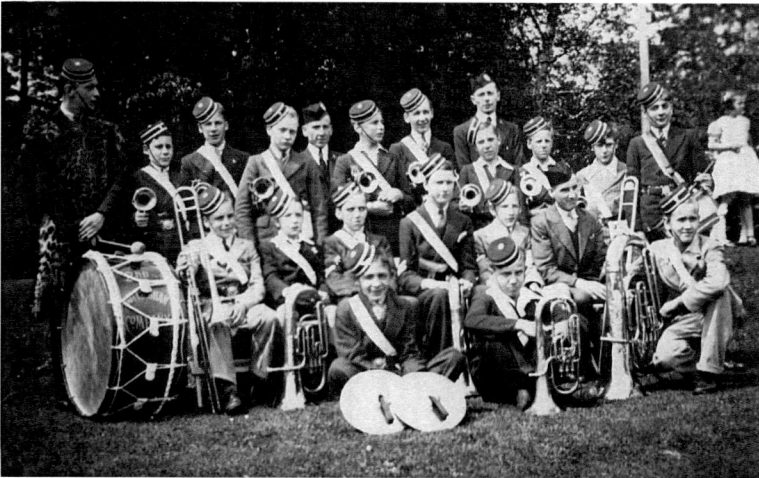

The band under bandmaster Leslie Hutchby in the mid 1930's.

The summer camp of 1938.

One of many successful football teams fielded between the war years.

The Charles Murray Years

Always faithful.

When Arthur Stevenson made known to the Trustees of the Club his intentions to leave, advertisements for a new Warden were circulated through appropriate magazines. Short listed applicants were interviewed at Edwalton Hall and it was agreed that the candidate who showed the most promise of success was Charles C. Murray.

Appointed Warden and Captain of the Club at a Trustee Meeting on the 9th of March, 1945, he attended the annual demonstration on the last Saturday of April as a guest and took over his responsibilities from Arthur Stevenson on the 4th of June 1945.

Charles Murray had been a member of The Boys' Brigade at Hawick both as a boy and an Officer, for twenty two years. He was authoritative, quick-witted, and resourceful. Driven by a strong commitment to the object and functioning of The Boys' Brigade, he set about his new role with alacrity and efficiency. During his period as Captain, the 2nd Company held its position of importance in the Nottingham Battalion and enjoyed many successes.

During the war, the Chapel St. Leonards camp site had not been used and had suffered damage. Borstal boys under the supervision of a local farmer were employed to make reparations and build a new cookhouse and camps were resumed from the summer of 1945. When not used by the 2nd Nottingham Company, the grounds were hired to other Companies, providing the Club with an additional source of revenue and providing opportunity for others to enjoy the facilities the site had to offer.

In the autumn of 1937, Captains Alex Michie and Charles Murray, members of the Hawick Boys' Brigade Officers' Council, had approached Robert Short, a highly experienced and enthusiastic piper who had developed his playing skills at the 1st Boys' Brigade Company in Thurso, with a view to setting up a Boys' Brigade Pipe Band at Hawick. Robert was delighted to accept the challenge and invited boys from the Hawick Companies to take up pipe and drum and form the Hawick Boys' Brigade Pipe Band. Within a few years they were immaculate and a pride to all involved.

Early in 1946, Charles Murray arranged the first of a series of visits of the Hawick Boys' Brigade Pipe Band to Nottingham. They were greeted with a civic reception and performed before crowds in the city centre before being entertained for a week at the Oliver Hind Boys' Club.

The following April, the 2nd Nottingham Company Silver Band and Gym Team returned the compliment by visiting and performing for their hosts in Hawick.

A holiday was scheduled for a party of boys to camp and tour around Holland in the summer of 1946. The day before their departure, Charles Murray was informed that the firm with which they had arranged the journey had been forced into liquidation. Not wanting to disappoint the boys, he made a last minute telephone call to his friends north of the border and the holiday was diverted to Scotland. The boys enjoyed a stay in dormitory accommodation in Hawick and the holiday included a trip to the Edinburgh Tattoo. From this time, throughout Charles Murray's Captaincy, a summer visit to Hawick became a regular and popular event.

Charles Murray turned another problem to his advantage when it was reported to him in 1946 that employees of the Nottingham Corporation had mistakenly dumped 80 tons of rubble intended for use at the Trent Leisure Park onto the Trent Lane Sports Ground.

According to the height of the river, the pitches at Trent Lane were prone to flooding and, in consequence, it was often uncertain whether sports fixtures would take place. To make amends for the mistaken dumping of rubble, it was agreed between Charles Murray and the embarrassed City Engineer that the rubble would be flattened out and that the Corporation would continue to dump and flatten rubble for a further ten years, raising the level of the ground by eight to nine feet. The operation was carried out in such a way that there was always one or two pitches available to accommodate team matches and the flooding problem was solved. The swimming pool section of the ground was given over to the Sea Cadets, who had the river bank secured and paid a nominal rent for the area.

On Sunday mornings, chairs were arranged in the band room, on the top floor of the Club premises, to accommodate the Bible class service. Towards the end of the war, Arthur Stevenson raised £600 for the purpose of building a small chapel adjacent to the Club to provide a more appropriate setting for Sunday worship. Charles Murray invested this sum to convert the basement room of the Club into a chapel. The work was completed in 1948 and the chapel was dedicated at a special service by Robert A. Wakely of the Castle Gate Congregational Church. Lecterns were donated by Mary Hind and Charles Murray.

Choreographing and directing a large number of boys in an extravaganza had been the province of Jack Bickerdike and several enthusiastic helpers for many years. In 1949, he directed about 60 boys from the 2nd Nottingham Company in a performance entitled 'Recreational Roundabout' at The Boys' Brigade demonstration at the Royal Albert Hall in London. An exiting and stimulating experience for the boys involved, he repeated the achievement four years later with an item called 'Twist and Turns'.

In 1952, Charles Murray was invited to attend a jubilee celebration to mark the fiftieth anniversary of the FDF, an equivalent organisation to The Boys' Brigade in Denmark that had been founded in 1902. Prior to attending the event, he hosted an Officer and three boys from Wisconsin, representing The Boys' Brigade in the United States of America. They were entertained as guests at the Oliver Hind Boys' Club for a week before accompanying Charles and four boys from the Club to the celebration Denmark.

The centenary anniversary of the birth of William Alexander Smith was marked by a Boys' Brigade demonstration at The Wembley Stadium in London in 1954. The 2nd Nottingham Company represented the Nottingham Battalion at the event by staging an item called 'Roman Chariots'.

This same year that saw the death of George Arthur Spick. He had joined the Club as a boy in 1909 and had been appointed to be an Officer by Oliver Hind at the end of the First World War. For many years he had proven to be a great asset to the Company in his role as Quartermaster. At the time of his death, his son David was a member of the Club. In his memory, his widow, Alice, donated covers for the lecterns in Company chapel.

The period of recovery after the war was a time of sweeping social change. The British Empire was dismantled; affordable appliances revolutionised household laundry and cleaning tasks; traditional crafts, such as furniture manufacture, were displaced by mass-production; people moved from inner city conurbations to new housing in the suburbs; television entertainment enticed people to spend their leisure hours at home. These trends had a detrimental effect upon the number of boys attending the Oliver Hind Boys' Club.

To counter the decline, Charles Murray visited local schools at the start of each session to speak about what the Club had to offer and encourage new members. He also introduced new activities, such as dance lessons given by William and Maggie Walkerdine (William Walkerdine had been a boy in the Dakeyne Street Lads' Club during the First World War; his son, David, at that time a boy in the Club, was later an Officer and, later still, the Secretary of the Board of Trustees) in an effort to attract more interest. But the size of the membership would never recover from what it had been before the war. Boys no longer clamoured for a place in shoe repair and woodwork classes; fewer were keen to form a line at drill parades; empty seats became a noticeable feature at Sunday Bible class.

The success of a club is determined by the size of its membership and this became a preoccupation that was to tax successive Captains of the Oliver Hind

Boys' Club over the following decades. But, for the remainder of Charles Murray's term, the Club maintained a good standard at sport, gymnastics, and band playing. At a Radio and Television Exhibition in London in 1955, boys from the Oliver Hind Boys' Club appeared on national television in a performance of 'Totem Tom Tom', a dance adapted from the musical show 'Rose Marie'.

Charles Murray's daughter Mary had married Albert Henshaw, a young Officer in the Club, in the summer of 1950. In the summer of 1957, the couple were blessed with a daughter. The birth coinciding with completion of alterations that were being made to the Company chapel, Lesley Mary Henshaw was baptised at the chapel re-dedication service, conducted by the Rev. Ronald Ward. The font used for the ceremony was donated by the Castle Gate Congregational Church.

The following September, Leonard Preston, a policeman and popular Officer of the Oliver Hind Boys' Club, was suddenly and tragically struck down and died of a heart attack while packing for a holiday with his wife and children. It was a prelude to a number of sad losses experienced at the Club.

The Captain's daughter, Mary Henshaw, affectionately known as Molly and leader of the Life Boys' unit at the Club, died suddenly of an asthma attack in the summer of 1959, two years after celebrating the birth of her daughter, Lesley Mary.

The following April brought news of the death of Mary Hind, aged sixty-four. Since her husband's death, she had continued, in her capacity as Chairman of the Trustees, to show a keen interest and concern for the well-being of the Boys' Club he had created. The responsibility of Chairman of the Trustees was taken over by her daughter, Mrs. Olive Weston, until 1963 and from that time by R. A. Jackson, President of the Nottingham Battalion followed, from the mid 1980's onward, by former boy and Officer in the Club, Reginald Green.

In November, Jack Bickerdike died from a heart attack at the age of fifty-seven. A keen and capable footballer and cricketer as a young man, he had taken over the duties of Nottingham Juvenile Probation Officer from Alfred Davidson and had later become Chairman and Secretary of the Nottingham Standing Conference of Youth Organisations. From August 1943 he took over the duties of North Midland Organiser of The Boys' Brigade. A charismatic youth leader who encouraged every boy to reach his full potential, he was highly respected and considered a friend and mentor by a great many boys. Alms dishes were dedicated to the Company chapel to commemorate his service to the Club.

The following year saw the death of Jack's friend and colleague, Harold Wright. He had been an diligent Officer and Secretary of the Oliver Hind Boys' Club for many years. He left a wife and son.

Charles Murray retired in 1963 having contributed eighteen years to managing the Oliver Hind Boys' Club through difficult times. At the annual demonstration preceding his retirement, the Hawick Boys' Brigade Pipe Band, who were special guests, gave a resounding demonstration of their own appreciation for the retiring youth leader.

The following summer, many guests were invited to attend the presentation that marked the end of his career. He received several gifts of his own choosing from Officers, boys, and friends of the Company. He had been a distinctive and popular Captain.

The Gymnastic Team with Captain Charles Murray on the Right and popular Officer Stan Lord on the left.

The Final Years at Dakeyne Street

Moving on.

David Taylor, the new Warden, was introduced by the Trustees to the Officers of the Club at a meeting in August 1963. He had previously been the Captain of a Boys' Brigade Company in Perth and had received a college training in youth work.

Faced with declining membership, changing social attitudes and competing diversions, his assignment was difficult.

The Dakeyne Street premises, which had been designed to accommodate large numbers of boys in the early part of the century, was aging and increasingly expensive to maintain, light and heat. Games and sports equipment and band instruments were worn and in a bad state of repair and there were no funds to replace them. Apart from donations from the Hind family, sources of income were limited to membership fees, revenues from campsite and equipment hire, canteen sales and government grants.

Respect for authority and enthusiasm for military style drill and medal attainment was waning. Some boys were beginning to treat the Club property with a measure of contempt not previously witnessed. It was clear that unless the Club could respond to changes taking place in the wider society, membership would continue to decline, possibly to a level where it would become unviable.

Early in 1964, a funeral service was held in the Company chapel for Leslie Hutchby who had been a member of the Club as a boy before the outbreak of the First World War and afterwards a prominent member of the Old Boys' Association, and a Company Officer. An adept and keen musician, he took over the role of Bandmaster in the mid 1930s and under his direction, the silver band maintained a high standard of performance, featuring at the Boy's Brigade annual demonstration at the Royal Albert Hall in London on several occasions. During the Second World War, in the absence of military bands, they played at the start and during the half-time interval at Notts County and Nottingham Forest football matches. In the summer months they entertained the public at county fetes. Leslie's sense of humour, natural warmth and enthusiasm for music inspired many instrumentalists to attain a high level of competence and perform to their best ability.

David Taylor presented plans to reverse the decline in Club membership. Unfortunately, while the other Officers recognised that changes were essential, he failed to convince them of the wisdom of the course he wished to adopt and came into conflict with them over his manner and approach. His plans stalled and the strength and morale of the Company declined at an even more rapid rate.

He grew despondent and resigned in November 1965 to take up a post as County Youth Officer in Dumfries. The Trustees asked the Officers to take over the running of the Club until a new Warden was appointed.

In the Spring of 1966, bad health forced Harry Shaw to retire from his position as Boys' Brigade Officer and Club caretaker. He had been a member of the team of Officers since the First World War and since 1929 had undertaken the role of caretaker, the duties of which position he shared with William Skellett, an original old boy of the Club, during the 1930's, and Harry Long, a retired Army Sergeant Major, from 1945. On alternative weeks, he spent every week-day evening supervising games in the Club from the control office. As an Officer he had attended nearly all camps, often working hard as camp cook. To show their gratitude for his immense contribution over the years, he was presented with a standard lamp at the annual demonstration for 1966. Sadly he died while on holiday shortly after retiring.

At a meeting before he left, David Taylor advised the Officers about sharing the responsibilities involved in running the Club. No one at the time indicating a desire to accept the position of Captain, it was agreed that an approach would be made to Derek Jacks to request him to take over the role.

Derek Jacks had been a boy and Officer in the 2nd Nottingham Company. As Colour-Sergeant, alongside Sergeant Albert Henshaw, who was later to marry Mary Murray, and eight other boys, he had been awarded The Boys' Brigade's highest award, the King's badge, in the annual demonstration and prize giving ceremony of May 1943. By the mid 1960's he was the Convener of the Southern District of the Nottingham Battalion of The Boys' Brigade. A regular speaker at Bible class services at the Oliver Hind Boys' Club, he showed particular brilliance in his mastery over the drill parade.

Derek took over the Captaincy in the winter of 1966 and over the next few years helped to strengthen and unify the Company. By unreservedly devoting his free hours to the needs of the Club, he inspired other Officers and boys and raised the morale of the Company.

Keith Vinerd, a young Officer who had succeeded Ralph Hopewell as first-aid instructor and was heavily involved in Duke of Edinburgh's Award activities, assisted in matters of correspondence and administration, as Company Secretary. David, the son of George Arthur Spick, who was now an Officer in the Club, assisted by liasing between Derek Jacks and the Board of Trustees.

During his period of tenure, David Taylor had obtained a surveyor's report upon the probable remaining life of the Dakeyne Street building. The estimate given was fifteen years and prompted the idea of acquiring new premises. The issue was added further impetus when it was announced that the building lay in the path of a proposed new motorway.

Negotiations took place between the Club Trustees and the Council out of which it was agreed that, in exchange for the existing property, the 2nd Nottingham Company would be provided with purpose built premises on Edale Road, off Sneinton Dale, on a long-term lease arrangement from the Council. While smaller than the existing accommodation, the new building would be more appropriate for the size of membership and easier and cheaper to maintain.

For two years, the Company operated as a happy unit under the Captaincy of Derek Jacks. Annual demonstrations were notable and representatives from the Company began once more to make favourable appearance at Battalion inter-Company competitions.

But the Captain was not endowed with the same level of authority as his predecessors, who were employed by the Education Committee, on issues surrounding the running and financing of the Club. In such circumstances, he insisted that all major decisions be discussed at Officers' meetings and action agreed by a consensus of opinion.

The system worked well until a disagreement between the Officers led to a breakdown. An impasse followed and, in 1969, Derek Jacks, Keith Vinerd, Peter Whiteley and others felt forced to resign. Boys' Brigade Officers of the highest calibre, all had given many years of invaluable service to the Company and their loss was considerable.

The Club Trustees promised the remaining Officers that they would employ a full-time Warden as soon as possible and, in the meantime, the Officers formed a committee, headed by Bernard Finch, to administer the Club. The annual camp at Chapel St. Leonards functioned as normal under the command of charismatic and popular Officer, David Walkerdine, and Bernard Finch and the committee of Officers successfully completed the 1969 season.

The new full-time Warden was John Garton. He had joined as a boy and had risen through the ranks to become Captain of 14th Nottingham Company of The Boys' Brigade between 1964 and 1968. In the year before his appointment at the Oliver Hind Boys' Club, he attended a college course in youth work.

His first session with the Club was dominated by the transfer of Company headquarters which was to take place on the 16th of October. At the last remembrance service at the Dakeyne Street premise, the games room was cleared and set out with seating to enable hundreds of old and present boys to take part in a service facing the war memorial. The address was given by Charles Murray and included a fond farewell to the old building.

The Legacy

The DAKO spirit.

The new premises of the Oliver Hind Boys' Club at Edale Road had a good sized games room, a craft room, a canteen area, a large hall with a stage and cupboards at one end, a number of small rooms including a changing room, a committee room, and a Captain's office close to the entrance, and an outside floodlit sports area. It was opened by the Earl of Elgin and Kincardine, J.P., D.L., President of The Boys' Brigade, on Friday the 16th of October 1970.

The Hawick Boys' Brigade Pipe Band visited for the occasion and performed before guests who included the Lord Mayor and Lady Mayoress of Nottingham.

After an inspection of the Company in the outside court there was a short service of dedication conducted by chaplain Rev. R. Duce, of Castlegate Congregational Church, after which a presentation was made by Charles Murray and a key to the premises was ceremoniously handed to the new Club Warden, John Garton.

Four years later, the Hawick Boys' Brigade Pipe Band returned to Edale Road to celebrate the eightieth anniversary of the formation of the 2nd Nottingham Company of The Boys' Brigade. Olive Weston, the second daughter of Oliver and Mary Hind, Charles Murray, the retired Captain, and Albert Ball, the senior Officer of the Club, were special guests for the occasion.

The job that Oliver Hind set out to do was complete. Thousands of boys had benefited from what he had provided. But times had changed. Education provided by the state was now all-embracing and comprehensive, This key element of Oliver Hind's objective was fully provided for by state schools and colleges.

Other social changes were having a dramatic effect upon The Boys' Brigade movement. Funding once provided by benefactors and well-wishers was now largely the gift of local authorities who had other interests and priorities to consider. For policy makers who were shaping the fabric of social life, The Boys' Brigade was seen as something of an anachronism. The first part of the name resonated with sexism and unequal opportunity; the second part seemed like an embarrassing hark-back to the time of the British Empire, best obliterated from the national consciousness. The Object 'to advance Christ's kingdom among boys and promote of habits of reverence, discipline, self-respect, and all that tends towards a true Christian manliness' clashed with modern, strictly-secular ideologies. Churches and chapels, to which the movement was closely associated, were also in decline, many being converted into shops and homes.

Coupling this with increased wealth and a widening range of diversions open to young people, it was inevitable that The Boys' Brigade movement would diminish in size.

The Oliver Hind Boys' Club became the Oliver Hind Youth Club. It withdrew from Boys' Brigade in 1984 and is now staffed by a small team of professional youth workers, who run youth club sessions several nights a week.

But there is a ray of the DAKO spirit that still shines brightly. It has been sustained by the constant endeavours of David Walkerdine and Tony Mee, both at one time boys and then Officers of the 2nd Nottingham Company at Dakeyne Street. David is now the Secretary of the Board of Trustees and head coach of the gymnastic team. Tony, in his capacity of caretaker, has maintained the nuts and bolts of the operation since the transfer from Dakeyne Street to Edale Road.

A high-quality gymnastic team had been an important part of the Oliver Hind Boys' Club tradition since its beginning. In 1931 the massed bands of the Sherwood Foresters Regiment beat a retreat in the Nottingham city centre before leading the 5th, 6th, 7th, and 8th battalions in full dress to the Notts County Football Ground where they staged a spectacular military performance before a crowd of 5000. The programme was opened by an exhibition of the Dakeyne Street gymnastic team.

After a lapse of a few years spanning the move from Dakeyne Street to Edale Road, David Walkerdine re-established a gym class in the mid 1970's. They featured at The Boys' Brigade annual demonstration at the Royal Albert Hall in 1976.

Since that time, among many memorable public performances, the 'DAKO Flying Angels', as they are called, have made eleven television appearances, performed at the World Gymnaestrada in Denmark in 1987 and Holland in 1991, attended the Spanish International Gym Festival at Grand Canary twelve times, performed three times at the Earls Court Royal Tournament, appeared in 'Wish

Upon A Star Charity' events at the Royal Concert Hall in Nottingham in 2001 and 2012, and featured in the Commonwealth Games Gymnastic Spectacular Gala of 2002. Winners of the British Gymnastic Association Ministrada at Liverpool in 1997, 2000, and 2003, they have acquired a glass-cabinet full of trophies.

In the early 1980s, David was approached by a mother whose boy was eager to join his class. In true DAKO spirit, he was happy to encourage any boy who seriously wanted to involve himself in gymnastics. The boy's mother went on to explain that her son had no legs from the knees down. It was a challenge but no impediment if the boy was keen enough. He was more than keen and soon became a valued member of the team.

As a young man, Richard Whitehead started a career as swimming instructor at the Clifton Leisure Centre in Nottingham. In 2006, he competed as part of the GB sledge hockey team at the Winter Paralympics in Turin. After this he went on to break the world record for athletes with a double leg-amputation, in the full and half marathon.

In August 2012, David Walkerdine carried the torch for the London 2012 Paralympic Games across London Tower Bridge on its route to the opening ceremony. He had been nominated for the honour by Richard Whitehead for his inspirational coaching and the encouragement given to him to achieve his best as a boy.

Richard went on to win gold medal in the 200 metres T42 Athletics event with a world record time of 24.38 seconds. In early 2013, he received a 'Member of the Order of the British Empire' award for his outstanding contribution to athletics.

A Modern Gym Team.

Postscript

Do a kindness often.

What has been presented in this short history is an account of people who dedicated themselves to helping the poor and disadvantaged attain a better standard of life. All shared a similar vision and each was inspired by the example and achievements of their forerunners.

Almost all were non-conformist Christians intent upon raising the hopes and aspirations of children trapped in a cycle of poverty, drudgery, degradation, and crime. They saw a desperate need and addressed it to the best of their power. Their reward was the joy of a loving parent watching an ailing child blossom and flourish.

Giving was central to their belief. Their model was the life of Jesus Christ as recorded in the first four books of the New Testament. It was a fundamental part of their faith that all are born equal and have equal potential to live useful and wholesome lives; that every child deserves equal consideration and, given opportunity, has capacity to excel in some sphere of life. Their ambition was to draw closer to building a heaven upon earth. They were successful because they were resolute, resourceful and driven by strong conviction.

In the twenty first century, free and comprehensive education for all is taken for granted. How much we owe the pioneers of free education for the poor for this is incalculable.

William Alexander Smith hit upon a formula for controlling boys in his Sunday Bible class by introducing them to the discipline practiced by the 1st Lanarkshire Rifle Volunteers and providing them with the type of healthy activities he was familiar with in the YMCA. Oliver Hind built upon this by providing educational opportunities, following the example of the Ragged School movement and Thomas Barnardo. 'Put the boy first' was a guiding principal for both men.

Like John Pounds, pioneer of free education for poor children (who no doubt would have made an inspiring Boys' Brigade Officer) they mixed socially with the boys in their care. Oliver Hind may have arrived at the Dakeyne Street Lads Club in a chauffer driven car but social distinctions were left outside the porch door when he entered the noisy games room.

Boys were provided with a wide range of opportunities and encouraged in every way to better themselves through application and endeavour. But it was a tough love. Rules were strict and strictly applied. It was not beyond Oliver Hind to wash a boy's face for him if he came looking dirty. The same boy would be saluted by the hand that had washed his face when he achieved his first award.

Esprit de corps and habits of discipline were key elements in maintaining cohesion amongst the hundreds of children involved. But it would be hard to overstate the level of trust and camaraderie engendered between the Officers and boys of such a club.

None of this jells with modern political dogma. Youth work has become the province of professionals, trained to follow tightly controlled standards in line with modern social and educational theory. What is gained is conformity and an assurance that all policy ascribed tick boxes are ticked. What is lost is the essence of what made clubs like the Oliver Hind Boys Club a wonderful place for thousands of boys.

The world has changed dramatically since the days of William Alexander Smith and Oliver Hind. It is rich beyond the imaginings of working class people a century ago and a place where those who direct social policy see little relevance in 'promoting habits of reverence, discipline, self-respect, and all that tends towards a true Christian manliness.'

But then again, the early twenty-first century in the United Kingdom has witnessed swathes of MPs fiddling their expenses; bankers playing fast and loose with other people's money and mis-selling to their customers; hospitals allowing patients to die for lack of care and attention; mentally ill and old people neglected and abused in care homes; journalists hacking into peoples private lives; solicitors hawking for trade, eager to turn a distressing accident into a nightmare; scammers, fraudsters, and thieves plaguing the old and vulnerable. It is a world of gang culture, drug abuse, binge drinking, an obesity epidemic, and an occasional social eruption and street riot. More than a century after Oliver Hind first opened the doors of the Dakeyne Street Lads' Club, the Oliver Hind Youth Club has to be secured by iron bars across windows and doors.

Perhaps, those men of the past may have had something in their method after all. Perhaps, even in this age of limitless choice and political correctness, there might be something to be said for the values propounded by those early proponents of The Boys' Brigade.

Early in its history, the Dakeyne Street Lads' Club was given the affectionate nickname, DAKO. This was subsequently expanded to provide the maxim "do a kindness often". Kindness is a word that has drifted out of common circulation but it encapsulates the character of Oliver Hind, who may have well conceived the adage. His thoughtful, positive and generous spirit permeated the club he created.

DAKO provided an environment where boys were encouraged to developed a character based on good manners, consideration for others (particularly those less well off), pride in appearance, integrity, and endeavour. In so doing, they learned skills and formed friendships that would hold them in good stead for the rest of their lives. Boys from successive generations of the same family passed through the same doors. It was a vibrant, positive, happy place run by dedicated volunteers who shared a vision for a better future, led by example, and provided thousands of boys with an uplifting and life-enriching experience.

God bless the good Samaritans who champion the cause of impoverished children.

God bless all who assist in their task.

God bless those who continue the work of The Boys' Brigade and similar youth organisations in spite of countless impediments put in their way.

God bless the boys who left a warm bed at 5.30am on a frosty Winter's morning to serve breakfast and deliver a Christmas cheer to six hundred destitute children at the Dakeyne Street Lads' Club.

God bless the boys who grew into hopeful young men whose lives were sacrificed in war.

God bless us all; each and every one.

Acknowledgements

This history would not have been written without contributions provided by the following witnesses to many of the events that have been described.

Alice and David Spick

Alice was the wife of George Arthur Spick and mother of David, boy and Officer in the Oliver Hind Boys' Club during the 1950s and 1960s. The family gave many years of valued service to the Club.

Albert Ball

Albert lived as a child on Dakeyne Street and joined the Lads' Club in 1911 at the age of twelve. His father was killed in the Great War in which Albert enlisted in the latter stages. Afterwards, he was employed by Oliver Hind as chauffer. Later, he became an Officer in the Oliver Hind Boys' Club. During the visit of the Duke of Gloucester, he acted as the Press Officer. He attended Bible class until well into the 1970's, in later times journeying from Edwalton where he and his wife lived in one of two almshouses that Oliver Hind had built in Edwalton in 1928 to commemorate the life of his parents and of his brother and nephew who had died in the Great War.

Charles C. Murray

Charles was the much respected Captain of the Club from 1945 to 1963.

Keith Vinerd

Keith was a boy and Officer in the Club during 1950's and 1960's. He ran a first-aid class and was a key figure in implementing the Duke of Edinburgh's Award. Since leaving the 2nd Nottingham Company and the 8th Nottingham Company, he has continued to play an important role within the Nottingham Battalion and has been the Executive Manager for the application of the Duke of Edinburgh's Award in Boys' Brigade throughout England and Wales.

David Walkerdine

David is an inspirational youth leader who for more than 50 years has motivated hundreds of boys to achieve their best. He continues to inspire, running the 'DAKO Flying Angels' gymnastic team and manages the Oliver Hind Youth Club as Secretary of the Trustees. He was awarded a British Empire Medal (BME) in 1991, in large part for his service to youth work in Nottingham.

Further References

The Boys' Brigade
http://www.boys-brigade.org.uk

The Nottingham Boys' Brigade
- http://nottingham.boys-brigade.org.uk

The Oliver Hind Youth Club
- http://www.nottinghamyouth.co.uk/index.aspx?articleid=10339

Papplewick Grange
- http://www.papplewick.org/local/history/papgrange.html

Edwalton Hall
- http://edwaltonlhs.co.uk/home.html

The Beeston Lads' Club
- http://www.beeston-notts.co.uk/ww1_bb.shtml

The Dakeyne Farm
 - http://www.dakeynefarm.com

The Battle of the Somme - July 1st 1916
 - http://www.therobinhoods.org.uk/gommecourt.shtml

The Battle of the Somme - September 27th 1916
- http://homepage.ntlworld.com/mike.briggs76/9th%20Btn.htm

The Dakeyne Street War Memorial
- http://www.thorotonsociety.org.uk/publications/articles/thedakoboys.htm